MARRIAGE
as equal partnership

MARRIAGE
as equal
partnership

Resolving a
New Testament
Paradox
in the Light
of Today's Debate

Dwight Hervey Small

BAKER BOOK HOUSE
Grand Rapids, Michigan

PHOTOLITHOPRINTED BY CUSHING - MALLOY, INC.
ANN ARBOR, MICHIGAN, UNITED STATES OF AMERICA

To

Those courageous colleagues in ministry
who share the vision of equal partnership in marriage,
yet who are unwilling
to relinquish the biblical teaching on headship

Contents

Introduction

Periodically there is a renewed interest in the question of what the Bible teaches about husband-wife roles in marriage. Today there is a strong resurgence of such interest, but along with it a sharp division of evangelical thought. The two opposing views center on the interpretation of Ephesians 5:21–33. The traditional view of headship-submission is being challenged in some important circles. Among the voices being heard are those of scholars, marriage therapists, popular conference speakers, and Christian feminists. At every echelon there are those who are advocating a new look at what Paul teaches in this respect.

Scripture is being reinterpreted, consciously or otherwise, to conform to an enlightened contemporary concept of equal-partnership marriage. Among university sociologists who teach courses in marriage and the family there is a uniform assumption that equal partnership is the only marriage system which serves the interests of a fair, just, and workable relationship between husbands and wives. This view alone seems to suit men and women who in every other respect are achieving equality in today's world. The biblical view seems outmoded, something we should relegate to the patriarchal era. The apostle Paul was a child of his times, his theological umbilical cord still attached to the thought patterns of the rabbinical schools. His view of liberty for women was especially myopic. Thus we must reconstruct the biblical data in terms of a more modern system for marriage. This we hear loudly.

Among biblical traditionalists there is an understandable fear that equal-partnership marriage undercuts the Scriptures. One of the widely-followed teachers of our day has a system of interpretation which builds around the notion of a "chain of command." While this view has gained many adherents, it has also brought a strong reaction among other teachers, both academic and lay, who feel it to be a distortion of New Testament teaching. And so the issue has given rise to a veritable debate. One voice that has emerged in a relatively recent period, a voice being heard with increasing seriousness, is that of the Christian feminists. To their voice we must give significant attention, for from them we have much to learn.

The rise of Christian feminism is rather recent, if we are to use such bench marks as publications and organizational endeavors. At this date of writing, the most recent and by far the most significant of the national conferences was that held at Fuller Theological Seminary, June 14–16, 1978, with the theme "Women and the Ministries of Christ." Following the conference, attended by some eight hundred women and a sprinkling of men, preliminary steps were taken to establish a national organization. Right-thinking men, it seems to me, can only applaud the emergence of a Christian women's movement. It follows exactly a decade after the identifiable beginnings of the feminist movement of our day, and well over a century after the rise of a feminist movement in modern times. We look to Christian women of God to provide strong leadership toward the legitimate, moderate goals of contemporary feminism.

In 1971 I first taught the Westmont College course entitled

"The Sociology of Women." The course was open to women students only; for five years I empathized with their desire that a woman professor might teach the course. The girls were delighted, however, that I seemed to share many of the objectives of a moderate feminism, sufficiently so to be considered on their side.

Well do I remember searching for adequate textbooks, and in 1971 there were pitifully few from secular presses, and none at all from Christian publishers. Christian feminism was embryonic, virtually invisible to evangelical eyes. Then in 1974 there appeared a book of such worth that it received the Christian Book of the Year Award from the book reviewers of *Eternity* magazine (mostly men, myself included!). It was *All We're Meant to Be* by Letha Scanzoni and Nancy Hardesty. That year I had three Christian books for my course, and this one was universally admired by the young women in my class. Perhaps they picked up on my own enthusiasm for the book. This was to be followed by another influential book, *Man as Male and Female* by an esteemed theologian, Paul K. Jewett. Since that time we've witnessed a continuing stream of books on the changing image and roles of women. And women's roles are certainly changing! As someone once commented, women today will hardly sit still for their portrait!

I love the story told by Nancy Reeves, an acclaimed author and lecturer who teaches at UCLA and holds membership in the California bar. Nancy tells of going to her grandmother's in San Diego each summer during her childhood. She was always fascinated by a weather barometer which had figures that emerged to indicate the prevailing conditions—one a little man, the other a little woman. But inasmuch as Nancy was always there during the mild weather of summer, she saw only the little man emerge. One day she asked her grandmother, "Grandma, where is the little woman?" "The little woman," replied the grandmother, "is in the house where she belongs." "But grandma," asked Nancy, "when will she come out of the house?" With a twinkle, the grandmother replied, "The little woman will come out of the house when there is a change in the weather.''

We should all be thankful for the change in the weather! Male chauvinism is not limited to the church of Jesus Christ, but it has been aided and abetted along the way by a male-dominated church. Rather than being in the foreranks of a liberation movement, the church has dragged its feet. Only now are we witnessing a long-overdue balancing of the books.

Not that I share all of the objectives of feminism (for reasons other than that I'm a male!), but I do feel there are roles that most definitely belong to women which have been denied them. It is thus that I come with some favorable credentials in the eyes of my feminist friends, and dare to question one of the fundamental interpretations of Scripture which has become current in their thinking, a position supported by at least one ranking theologian and a growing number of popular writers.

Ephesians 5:21–33 is crucial to any understanding of the structure and functioning of the marriage relationship, and the marriage roles of husband and wife are at the very heart of the feminist's concern for equality. It is as though this relationship is the touchstone. The final objective, namely, equal-partnership marriage, I share and have advocated in my marriage course and in publications for many years. What gives me great concern is the manner in which this position is reached through the interpretation of this key New Testament passage. It is thus with some sense of reluctance, yet with an urgent sense of the need to avoid scriptural error, that I call for a reexamination of this interpretation. My own position includes that of the traditionalist as far as one must so interpret the structure of headship-submission in Ephesians 5:21–33. But I see the mode of its outworking as a pattern of mutual servanthood in love, and thus of equally shared submission one to the other. This must be qualified, of course, and this we seek to do as well. The issue in question becomes a paradox of Scripture, and it seems to me that this is what is lost to view by many interpreters on both sides.

With my best wishes for continuing success for my friends in the Christian feminist movement, I submit this contribution to the present debate. As we hammer out a position in concert one with the other, may the Lord of Scripture (the Lord of Christian feminism!) be pleased to lead us closer to His truth.

So, in response to the query, "Are the Christian feminists right?" my initial answer is, "For the most part, yes! As for their interpretation and application of Ephesians 5:21–33, well, let's see."

Unless there is indication to the contrary, the Scripture quotations are from the Revised Standard Version.

A Partnership of Equals Within God's Appointed Order

1

Within the past few years a debate has arisen among evangelical Christians, especially among Christian feminists, as to the proper interpretation of marital roles in Ephesians 5:21–33. The traditional interpretation of this passage (and the parallels in Colossians 3 and I Peter 3) is to see a hierarchy of positions occupied by husband and wife. This hierarchy is for the purpose of establishing a marital role pattern with a delegation of authority. Hierarchy means simply that *one person stands under another in respect to the pattern of authority in their relationship.* It is a matter of *order* primarily, sometimes involving status. However, it does not imply, as many claim, superiority over against inferiority. Nor does the biblical outworking of marital hierarchy place one spouse at a disadvantage before the other. That there can be a beautiful unfolding of an equal-partnership marriage is something I maintained in the book *Design for Christian Marriage* written twenty years ago. That position is the one I hold today, but, as this book shall accent, for more deeply considered reasons. In this matter I differ from some highly esteemed colleagues.

A superficial understanding of Ephesians 5:21–33 inevitably leads Christian wives to think Paul is putting them down, casting them into a position of inferiority, while granting their husbands carte blanche to dominate and direct their every move. Too many wives have experienced this very thing, only to find that such domination and oppression are intolerable. Male domination in marriage is destructive to any happiness or creativity. No wonder wives accuse the apostle of male chauvinism, and all too eagerly relegate his teaching to the culture in which he was socialized.

Marriage as we know it today, if it is to be happy and harmonious, must develop around husband-wife roles that are truly complementary and individually satisfying. There must be a contribution of each spouse's strengths to the other's weaknesses in a mutual ministry. Each of the pair has his own individual gifts to be expressed, his own potential to be fulfilled. On one hand, there is to be growth in a couple's unity; on the other hand, growth in their individuality. Each spouse must serve to facilitate the growth of the other. Such growth and personal benefit must come in equal shares. Neither spouse is to be assigned an inferior status, nor made subject to the dominating control of the other. In our times, the social, economic, and intellectual emancipation of women has its correlate in the widespread rejection of any arrangement which accords husbands a superior place. We can no longer speak of "man's world" or "woman's place." Equalitarian marriage is a growing reality the world over, and with it has come a radical reexamination of the marital order set forth in the New Testament.

Order in Marriage

As Christians, we must first suppose that the Divine Author would provide an order for the organization and functioning of any social institution such as marriage. Within that order we would expect explicit guidelines for the appropriate living out of the partnership. Moreover, that order with its means of implementation would then constitute a divine mandate for all Christian couples. We would expect, further, that the principles would be unchanging, although the implementation would change with the cultural settings of different times and places, and with the developing insights and abilities of both men and women.

To fulfill such a mandate would mean experiencing marital happiness and harmony under the blessing of God; to reject that mandate would mean experiencing the opposite—the loss of God's blessing. Not that this necessarily means the inability of couples to achieve relatively good marriages, only that the ultimate means of happiness and harmony wouldn't be present. No matter how fine, marriage could not be all that God wishes to make it. Thus our present quest is to explore God's appointed order and its implementation, to see the beauty and symmetry of His wise pattern for Christian couples.

The crux of the question has to do with the meaning of the husband's headship and the wife's subjection to it. Beyond that lies the further question as to whether these roles are indeed applicable to today, or only reflect Paul's instructions to Christian couples within the history and culture of the first century. Is this hierarchical structure Paul's concession to what was expected in his day? Were his thinking and teaching conditioned by his rabbinic background? Was he unknowingly restricted in his insights on social relationships because he happened to live in a patriarchal society? Was he simply perpetuating the male dominance entrenched in Judaism? Since male dominance was something that resulted from the fall and hence was eradicated in redemption, is the headship of husbands in marriage to be reversed? These are the critical questions in the current debate.

The Modern Attack on the Hierarchical Interpretation

These urgent questions have gained prominence in recent years with the appearance of a number of books, some by very fine leaders in the Christian feminist movement. The common belief is that marriage, if it is to be a partnership of equals, is impossible within a hierarchical structure. To their way of thinking, since equal partnership seems beyond any question in terms of modern life, and since for them it seems rooted by implication in Galatians 3:28, Paul's embarrassing teaching on headship must be managed in some way. Alongside the thinking of contemporaries, Paul seems hopelessly out of step.

One way to deal with the supposed problem is to say that for any number of understandable reasons Paul was wrong— simply wrong. This is the position of Fuller theologian Paul Jewett. Not that his exegesis of Scripture or understanding of the meaning of hierarchy can be faulted. Not at all. In this respect he does us the service of a clear exposition. But then, having established the biblical basis for the hierarchical view, he turns around and rejects it out of hand.

A second way to deal with the supposed problem is not to say that Paul was wrong, but that the church in its traditional theology has wrongly interpreted him. In support of this position is proposed an alternative interpretation. In the process, Paul's terms and the marital roles they represent are radically altered. Great stress is laid upon two passages of Scripture.

Ephesians 5:21 is said to be the overarching key to everything that follows ("Be subject to one another out of reverence for Christ"). As we shall see, this foundational verse is not only given its rightful prominence (having been for so long neglected in traditional expositions), but is then elevated to such a controlling position as to render headship and subjection of little if any significance at all. This passage is said to teach mutual subjection, which in turn demands total equality in marriage roles. Any inequality of roles suggested by headship-subjection is ruled out as a sub-Christian view. Not ruled out, however, on the ground of our more enlightened cultural development today, but on theological grounds which incorporate the notion that all spouses are equal in every way because they are created equally in the image of God and are equally the objects and beneficiaries of redemption. In this view, social justice demands that there be no social distinctions. This is the new perspective to be applied to biblical understanding.

The second passage employed to overturn the notion of marital hierarchy is Galatians 3:28 ("There is neither Jew nor Greek, there is neither slave nor free, there is neither male nor female; for you are all one in Christ Jesus"). If there is a contradiction between this passage and Ephesians 5 (and some teach that there is), then the principle which is less acceptable from our contemporary standpoint (namely, hierarchy), must be disavowed in favor of the more acceptable (namely, equal marriage). We make that choice. This means, in effect, that in Christ all persons are equal in every way, and such distinctions as race, class, and sex no longer have any bearing on social roles—whether outside or inside of marriage. Galatians 3:28, which comes from the same apostle, is judged to be his more mature thinking, the implication being that marriage is an equal partnership in every possible respect. This seems attractive and reasonable enough. But there is a fallacy easily overlooked, and to that we shall pay some attention shortly.

Equal Marriage Within a Hierarchical Structure

Those who hold the hierarchical view are termed traditionalists, with the obvious inference that this is old and outmoded, and that traditionalists are unable to hold to equal partnership in marriage. While to some this seems self-evident, it happens to be erroneous. Modern traditionalists see a fundamental paradox, but no contradiction, in opting for equal marriage within a hierarchical structure. They see it as a truly complementary relationship with a beautiful symmetry and equality of cooperation. Yet all of this is maintained within the biblical order of Ephesians 5:21–33. This equal partnership is possible, of course, whenever there is an acceptance of the conditions God places upon husbands especially. What this means in practice is that loving and mutual service is mandated for both spouses.

Christ Himself becomes the role model for both spouses. The nature of His headship, on one hand, and the nature of His subjection to the Father, on the other hand, make Him the model for both husband and wife. And not only is He the model, but also the enabler! Apart from that model, that enabling, the result will always be some form of overbearing male dominance, and some form of undercutting female resistance. Understandably, historical examples of failure and particularly perversion of headship have encouraged wives to believe that the pattern itself is either unbiblical or unworkable.

Contemporary Teaching Reexamined and Found Wanting

Unquestionably, the idea of the husband as the head to whom the wife is subject may become all the more objectionable under Bill Gothard's terminology, "chain of command." This very phrase tends to distort the truth of Scripture, for it is military terminology. And as if this were not bad enough, Gothard also refers to the husband as the hammer, the wife as the chisel, and the children as nonparticipating objects upon which the hammered chisel does its work. This infers an active role for the husband, a passive role for the wife and children. The wife is not part of the "command" in the chain of command. Besides being biblically warped, this language inspires a dangerous mindset.

Herbert Miles in the book *Husband-Wife Equality* rejects the hierarchical passages and thus is guilty of a one-sided emphasis.[1] He delights in reiterating, "A committee of two has no chairman." But of course we are not talking about a committee, for marriage can hardly be likened to a committee. Furthermore, we are not considering human ideas about marriage, but that which God directs in His Word. Miles falls into an unacceptable

---

1. Herbert J. Miles and Fern H. Miles, *Husband-Wife Equality* (Old Tappan, NJ: Fleming H. Revell, 1978).

hermeneutic, focusing on passages which emphasize equality (for example, I Peter 3:7, "joint heirs of the grace of life"), while ignoring or misinterpreting passages which speak of the headship and subjection of marital hierarchy. He fails to understand that both principles must work together.

Paul Jewett, in his book *Man as Male and Female*, also rejects the hierarchical pattern, but not because he thinks Scripture doesn't teach it. On that he is quite positive. As for Ephesians 5, he writes that "within the limitations of the marriage bond, one can hardly conceive of a more clear and emphatic statement of hierarchy."[2] And for those like Virginia Mollenkott who insist that hierarchy necessarily means that one person is superior and the other inferior, Jewett is worthy of hearing: "The concept of hierarchy, to be sure, does not in itself entail superiority and inferiority, but only that some are *over*, others *under*; some exercise authority, others submit to it."[3] He concludes his examination of Ephesians 5 by conceding, "Obviously, then, the marriage relation is not a matter of mutuality as between equal partners."[4] He can mean, of course, only that a hierarchical structure doesn't assign equal roles to the two partners in terms of authority-responsibility. What Jewett fails to see, it would seem, is that within the unequal role structure there is nonetheless full equality of opportunity for personal participation, growth, and fulfillment. There is no implied inequality of personal sharing in the daily conduct of life together.

Jewett's concessions are as interesting as his denials. For all his labor to overturn the validity of Paul's teaching concerning the hierarchical pattern, he hedges his position with this acknowledgment:

As we have said, in rejecting the subordination of the woman to the man, we are not rejecting hierarchy as such, but only an

---

2. Paul K. Jewett, *Man as Male and Female* (Grand Rapids: Eerdmans, 1975), p. 58.
3. Ibid., p. 71.
4. Ibid., p. 59.

expression of it that falls short of the ideal established by Christian revelation. As a matter of fact, the Christian vision of reality is hierarchical in a very fundamental way. For example, what one may call the "hierarchy of grace" in Paul's thought cannot be doubted from a Christian point of view. By the "hierarchy of grace" we mean, according to Christian doctrine, that God is the source of all authority (Rom. 11:33); that the Son of God voluntarily humbled himself as the Messiah and Savior (I Cor. 15:28), becoming obedient to his Father in all things even unto death, yea, the death of the cross (Phil. 2:6–8); that because of this obedience the Son has been highly exalted in his messianic office and made head over all things to the church (Phil. 2:9–11); and that for this reason all Christians are subject to him who is the head, freely confessing him as Lord and Savior (Rom. 10:9). This hierarchy consisting of God, Jesus the Christ, and the Christian believer, to which Paul appeals in his argument in I Corinthians 11:3, is at the very center of Christian revelation.[5]

Unfortunately, in developing his argument for rejecting the hierarchical pattern for marriage, Jewett expresses a bias against the reliability of Paul, saying that Paul "reflects the historical limitations of his Christian insight,"[6] that he "did not see the implications of his own great declaration," referring to Galatians 3:28. Jewett speaks of "the apostle's ambivalent view," and suggests, "Whatever limitations one may perceive in Paul's view of the wife's subjection . . . as a whole he had remarkable insight for a former Jewish rabbi."[7]

This same questionable approach is employed by Virginia Mollenkott in her book *Women, Men, and the Bible*. She, too, rejects the hierarchical pattern, not on the basis of offering a new interpretation of what Paul said (although she takes a nontraditional tack here also), but on the ground that Paul was wrong. Like Jewett, she concludes that Paul was conditioned by his rabbinic background. "Like us all," she writes, "Paul was a product of his own culture. He sometimes yielded to his own

---

5. Ibid., p. 133.
6. Ibid., p. 138.
7. Ibid., p. 142.

conditioning or, as is probable in this case, felt forced to accommodate his arguments to the prejudices of his readers. . . . Let us, then, courageously recognize that Paul's human limitations do crop up in his arguments undergirding female subordination."[8] With approval she quotes Calvin Roetzel: "It would be remarkable indeed if Paul did not reflect some of the prejudice, superstition, and bias of his own time."[9] Must not evangelicals object to this understanding of apostolic authority and biblical inspiration?

But Mollenkott goes further; she also faults the apostle's motivation: "To have used overt terminology of husbandly submission to the wife would have totally alienated people who were conditioned to male supremacy. They would have been so shocked that they would have rejected everything else in the gospel message."[10] Thus, Peter and Paul were "trying to avoid distracting the Jews from the gospel message by too radical a reaction against Jewish customs."[11] The apostles delivered only "expected remarks." All of this suggests that what we have is the apostle deviously calculating the effect of his message, unwilling to risk any dangerous reactions, or, as she puts it, "a sudden and catastrophic challenge to the whole social order."[12]

Since when have we charged the apostles with trying to avoid Jewish reaction? Can we cavalierly explain away Paul's teaching by questioning his motivation? What about the inspiration of the Holy Spirit in Paul's writing? Does not this questioning of Paul's motivation do violence to our understanding of his divinely-given authority as an apostle? Does it not raise the question as to what else in the New Testament may be subject to the defect of historical limitation, rabbinic conditioning, partial human insight, or just plain accommodation to the customs and culture of

---

8. Virginia Ramey Mollenkott, *Women, Men, and the Bible* (Nashville: Abingdon, 1977), p. 101.
9. Ibid., p. 105.
10. Ibid., p. 30.
11. Ibid.
12. Ibid.

the time? What seems the deeper danger in all this is that it makes Scripture subject to the equally limited and biased opinions of the interpreter who stands in his or her own culture and history. But even apart from this, the argument of Ephesians 5 is directly based on a Christological foundation, and hence clearly transcends culture.

Our contention is that marriage, as a mutual partnership of equals in action, is not at all incompatible with the hierarchical order for marriage. We do not have to manipulate Scripture to make it say what it doesn't say, or to deny that the apostles were right. It is not a problem of either we accept the hierarchical structure and deny equal-partner marriage, or we accept equal-partner marriage and deny the hierarchical structure.

The Place of Power in Marriage

Whether authority has a place in marriage is a basic question. Every social institution known to man is oriented to authority in some manner. Marriage is no exception. Elisabeth Elliot expresses it well:

> Acceptance of the divinely ordered hierarchy means acceptance of authority—first of all, God's authority and then those lesser authorities which He has ordained. A husband and wife are both under God, but their positions are not the same. A wife is to submit herself to her husband.... The mature man acknowledges that he did not earn or deserve his place by superior intelligence, virtue, strength, or amiability. The mature woman acknowledges that submission is the will of God for her, and obedience to this will is no more a sign of weakness in her than it was in the Son of Man when He said, "Lo, I come—to do Thy will, O God."[13]

In this same connection, Elliot makes an acute observation: "The image of God could not be fully reflected without the

---

13. Elisabeth Elliot, *Let Me Be a Woman* (Wheaton, IL: Tyndale House, 1976), p. 141.

elements of rule, submission, and union."[14] Of the several reasons why this is true, there is one which, though important, is often neglected:

> One of God's purposes in arranging things as He has is the restraint of power. Both men and women are given special kinds of power, and each kind needs to be specially restrained.... As man's power over woman is restrained by love, woman's power over man is restrained by the command to submit.[15]

Whether we argue for inherently determined factors or for the effect of socialization, we can speak in generalized terms of the unique emotional and sexual powers of woman, the physical and aggressive powers of man. How easily man can coerce, woman manipulate! Now, of course, there are wide individual differences, and it is somewhat fallacious to generalize these differences and fall into stereotypes. But it is beyond question that individual men and women bring to marriage their own uniquely individual forms of power. So each marriage is a unique power structure in itself. But whatever its expressed form of power, God's order is designed for the restraint and control of those powers. And wherever there are mutual love and service in the fear of Christ, one of the chief effects will indeed be a restraint of power. But since spouses voluntarily grant the Lord the prerogative of restraining power, such mutual submission to Him becomes a form of personal strength.

It is not too much to say that the temptations to power, together with the restraining disciplines of love and service, are necessary components in the building of moral, social, and spiritual character. This is the way toward maturity in marriage. God knows what is needed for our growth, as well as for our facilitating the growth of our spouses. For this reason He places the most intimate of relationships—marriage—within a given order. He grants both husband and wife their own unique strengths and weaknesses. He allows their unique temptations

---

14. Ibid., p. 60.
15. Ibid., p. 149.

for power, appoints their corresponding roles, then directs their ministry to each other. This is God's method of managing what might be called the *complementarity of power* within marriage. The hierarchical order provides *the mode* for marital relating; love and servanthood provide *the means,* as we shall see. Together, the design leaves nothing to be desired. This is exquisitely captured in the prayer of Sir Alexander Paterson which Elliot cites: "Make us masters of ourselves, that we may be the servants of others."[16]

Reference is often made to Letha and John Scanzoni's *Men, Women, and Change,* a sociology textbook on marriage. Four types of marital power relationships are outlined. Husband and wife may relate as (1) *owner-property,* (2) *head-complement,* (3) *senior partner-junior partner,* (4) *equal partner-equal partner.*

This is an excellent paradigm, but it is particularly appropriate to non-Christians as it stands. For the Christian couple, the ideal is no less than the *equal partner-equal partner* relationship. But they still must work this out within God's appointed order of headship and submission. With the model and enabling power which Christ supplies, this is not at all an impossibility. The Christian view combines the concepts of *head-complement* and *equal partner-equal partner,* and does so without contradiction. We shall put this to the proof as we go along.

Theologian Karl Barth understood this perfectly:

> The fact that the relationship is not one of reciprocity and equality, that man was not taken out of woman but woman out of man, that primarily he does not belong to her but she to him, and that he thus belongs to her only secondarily, must not be misunderstood. The supremacy of man is not a question of value, dignity or honour, but of order. It does not denote a higher humanity of man. Its acknowledgment is no shame to woman. On the contrary, it is an acknowledgment of her glory, which in a particular and decisive respect is greater than that of man.[17]

---

16. Ibid., p. 153.
17. Karl Barth, *Church Dogmatics* III/1, trans. J. W. Edwards, O. Bussey, and Harold Knight (Edinburgh: T. & T. Clark, 1961), pp. 301–03.

Barth argues that so long as the wife's subordination is viewed as it was in creation, it could involve no humiliation on her part, or dominance on the husband's part. But once mankind's relationship to God was disturbed by sin, the first couple's relationship to each other was also disturbed. Intimacy made them vulnerable to each other's powers. Their complementarity became competition and contradiction. A power struggle grew out of the tension. All of this led to the conflict of blind dominion on man's part and jealous zeal for emancipation on the woman's part. Man's position was debased to the power of coercive tyranny, while woman's position was debased to the power of subtle manipulation. Harmony was turned into disharmony, to envy and subversion. There was no inner restraint of powers! And it was woman who, throughout history, was to suffer most from the disorder.

The Biblical Ideal

What stands out so beautifully in the New Testament is not evidence of the reversal of God's order in Ephesians 5 by some other directive. It is the informing of the divine order with principles for its proper functioning, which demonstrates that the headship-subjection pattern of Ephesians 5 serves the supreme welfare of both spouses. The husband-wife roles merge into a beautiful symmetry of mutual love and service. If this is the case, then why reject the hierarchical order in which God says this beautiful symmetry is possible?

While I do not share all of the views of Larry Christenson, I find the discussion of marital order in his recent book *The Christian Couple* to be very incisive:

Status and subordination are two separate issues in Scripture. . . . It is possible to be subject to one who is superior . . . believers are subject to Christ. . . . Or there can be subordination among equals: Christ is equal to God yet subject to God; believers who are equal to one another . . . are admonished to be ''subject to one another." . . . One can even be called to subordinate himself to someone who is inferior, as Christ submitted to Pontius Pilate. Status is a sovereign determination of God. . . . Headship and subordination are sovereign appointments of God. . . . The fact that wives are told to be subject to their husbands tells us nothing about their status. If we had that statement only, we wouldn't know whether they were inferior, equal, or superior to their husbands. . . . The Bible makes no distinction between men and women as to their status. "In Christ there is neither male nor female" (Gal. 3:28). They are "joint heirs of the grace of life" (I Pet. 3:7). . . . In regard to the question of status and subordination, the relationship of husband and wife is analogous to that of the Father and the Son. . . . A wife has the same kind of relationship with her husband that Christ has with God: she is equal to her husband; she is subject to her husband. The stigma of inferiority is as inappropriate to the wife as it is to Christ. On the other hand, just as certainly as Christ is subject to God, a wife is subject to her husband.[18]

For all that we must understand in the general command to be subject to one another, there is, then, this basic, fundamental structure of hierarchy in marriage. No suggestion exists anywhere in the New Testament that this has been or ever shall be rescinded—some Christian feminists to the contrary. The concept of headship is neither renounced nor reversed! The husband is always the head, the wife never. With regard to headship, the wife is subject to her husband in a way that he can never be subject to her—notwithstanding interpretations of mutual subjection to the contrary! It is, rather, in practical reality that the husband is indeed subject to his wife in a most genuine way. His subjection to her is not a matter of altering positions, but is the practical outworking of love! To this he is called! His subjection is directed to her person, and is a matter of love; her subjection is directed to his position, and is a matter of obedience. This is God's declared order, and it is not our prerogative to tamper with it.

18. Larry Christenson, *The Christian Couple* (Minneapolis: Bethany Fellowship, 1977), pp. 117–18.

I concur with Larry Christenson when he writes, "When we ask which type of relationship 'will work,' we must remember that only that works which has God's blessing upon it, and that which has God's blessing is that which He Himself has commanded and ordered."[19]

As husbands and wives, we are what God says we are—equal; as husbands and wives we accept the service God has appointed to us—in either headship or subjection. Whether or not this suits our particular philosophy of what contemporary marriage should be, the only proper response of the Christian is obedience. And whether or not we recognize it, the fact remains that God has established this order for our highest good.

In her book *The Committed Marriage,* Elizabeth Achtemeier says of Ephesians 5:21–33:

> The passage is ingenious. It has preserved the traditional view of the male as the head of the family, but that headship is a function only, not a matter of status or superiority. The understanding of headship and of the wife's relation to it has been radically transformed. There is no lording over the other here, no exercise of sinful power, no room for unconcern or hostility toward the other. Instead there is only the full devotion of love, poured out for the other in imitation of Christ's faithfulness and yearning and sacrifice for his church, and of the church's like response to him. In short, there is here that total and loving commitment . . . the most perfect pattern for Christian marriage.[20]

It is good that husband-wife equality is a prominent concern in our time. We are wholeheartedly in favor of extending that equality to every facet of daily living. But there is one thing we must remember: Equality is one principle among others; it doesn't stand alone and unqualified as though it were the only word of God to us. It is only one part of the divine equation. It is entirely true; it is not the entire truth. And what humanly seems

---

19. Ibid., p. 35.
20. Elizabeth Achtemeier, *The Committed Marriage* (Philadelphia: Westminster Press, 1976), pp. 86–87.

contradictory to us may be a divine paradox. Thus, in Ephesians 5:21–33 it becomes obvious that husbands and wives are equal in every respect save one—authority and responsibility. As we've begun to see, this inequality in authority-responsibility is mitigated inasmuch as the husband carries this as his own peculiar burden before the Lord. It is not to be envied, only supported prayerfully. What truly does alleviate all wifely fears is the call to mutual love and Christlike service at the heart of this paradoxical relationship. Its beauty, symmetry, and fairness unfold as we place ourselves within these special conditions under which biblical marriage functions.

The simple, unqualified statement of Ephesians 5:21, a statement nowhere repeated or expanded upon, is, "Be subject to one another out of reverence [literally, fear] for Christ." Undisclosed in the general statement itself is the manner in which the call to mutual subjection is to be implemented in differing social relationships. Typically, traditionalists read too little in this foundational verse, feminists too much. We must ask what limits are intended to qualify the general command, "Be subject to one another."

Does the apostle mean to say, "Be equally subject to one another in every respect"? Or is he saying, "Take turns being subject to one another"? Should we take the statement to mean, "I'll be subject to you in this area, if you are subject to me in that"? Could Paul mean that mutual subjection should make no room for different roles, no room for any division of authority and responsibility? To adopt any one of these explanations is to read into the statement what is not there and to make an arbitrary choice of interpretation, probably to suit one's predetermined bias as to what a relationship should be.

The answer to our question, plainly, does not lie in the statement itself. We must look elsewhere for the manner in which the apostle intends his statement to be qualified. Does he give us any specific illustrations? We do not have to look far! We are immediately provided with illustrations of what he means. Curiously, the sentence following verse 21 does not contain a verb, but relies on the verb "be subject" in verse 21. Literally, then, we read, "Be subject to one another out of reverence for Christ, wives to your husbands. . . ." In other words, the statement in verse 21 leads directly to an inseparable application. But more than that, the qualifying words run on through verse 9 of chapter 6! So if we really want to know what some of the applications of verse 21 are, all we need do is to read on and we have three illustrations immediately! And what confronts us first of all is the hierarchical order for being subject to one another in marriage!

In the succeeding verses, as we've mentioned, three quite fundamental relationships are considered. The first two (husbands-wives; parents-children) are relationships rooted in the orders of creation, the third (masters-slaves) is not. Paul mentions the third for the simple reason that it was an existing relationship in his day. Paul is not concerned here to argue for its continuance or discontinuance; he is concerned for the proper Christian role within the existing structure. Still, the principle being established is the same for all three of these relationships: *there is authority invested in some, subjection required of others;* there is no hint whatever of interchangeable roles! If equal roles were what Paul had in mind, then these illustrations would only lead us astray. But obviously this is not the case.

So, take the first relationship to be illustrated, marriage. In the bill of particulars, Paul assumes that the man plays the role of husband, the woman the role of wife. The husband has a special call to headship, the woman to subjection. But within his special call, the husband is told that headship is to be expressed in a way man had never dreamed of before—in love! To undergird his call to husbands, Paul is moved by the Spirit to introduce an analogy which is fundamental to the Christian perception of marriage. *The husband stands in relationship to his wife as Christ stands in relationship to His church. The wife stands in relationship to her husband as the church stands in relationship to Christ.* Christ is the Head of the church, the husband head of the wife. The roles are not the same; they are different; they must be! But, again, what brings about an equal-partnership marriage for all practical and real purposes is the call to love and service. Love implies service, and service implies love; *this is the divine paradox!*

It should be clear by now that the rationale for equal-partner marriage cannot be found in verse 21 of Ephesians 5. Further on I shall show that it cannot be established on the basis of Galatians 3:28 either, as so many insist today. Yet I would contend no less than others for equal-partner marriage. Its rationale, it seems to me, is based on the mutual functioning of *Christlike, self-giving love* (which husbands translate into caring for and service to their wives), and *subjection* (which wives model after Christ's relationship to His Father, and the church's relationship to Christ, and which for wives translates into love-in-action toward their husbands).

The starting point for the husband, you see, is headship, for the wife subjection. But the end result for both is the same— *loving subjection and service.* From different initial positions, both spouses are brought to render the same ministry to each other, a ministry destined to bring harmony and happiness in equal shares. The major difference is simply that husbands are given an ultimate responsibility for the achievement of all this.

The paradox, simply put, is this: Husbands and wives are different but equal; they are equal but different. They have equal personhood, equal status, equal place, equal expression of gifts and individuality, equal spiritual standing, equal voice and vote. They are equal in everything but in divinely appointed authority and responsibility.

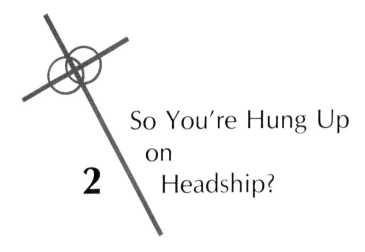

So You're Hung Up on Headship?

2

In Ephesians 5:23 we read, "For the husband is the head of the wife as Christ is the head of the church." Before we can understand the meaning and significance of the husband's headship, we must first understand the nature of the model, namely, the headship of Christ.

There are seven pertinent uses of the term *head* in the Pauline Epistles (I Cor. 11:3; Eph. 1:22; 4:15; 5:23; Col. 1:18; 2:10; 2:19). As to learning how Christ came to be Head, we are confined to a single passage, Ephesians 1:22. There we are told that God "has put all things under his feet and has made him the head over all things for the church." He became *Head* when the Father *made Him Head over all things for the church*. This clearly indicates that headship is a position of status or rank. It is a position of preeminence, of authority and responsibility. It is given in virtue of something accomplished, and given as part of an established order. The headship of Christ is a position to which He was appointed in virtue of His redeeming work.

The majority of pertinent references to headship are found in Ephesians and Colossians. There Christ's position of authority as the exalted Lord receives special emphasis. He is seen invested with all authority and power; this is the dominant message of both epistles.

The Two Meanings of "Headship"

In our time a confusing and one-sided interpretation of the metaphor of headship is emerging, its advocates saying that headship means something quite different from what we've just indicated. This is due to the fact that when the term *head* is used figuratively, it may mean one of two different things. These meanings are established in our standard Greek lexicons. The two meanings are not to be ranked as primary and secondary; rather, the precise meaning being employed is to be determined solely on the basis of the context in which the term is found. Christian feminists are among those most likely to choose the meaning which is removed from connotations of status or rank, preeminence, authority and responsibility. Instead, they think of headship as, say, the head of a river—the *origin,* or *source of being.* This, of course, provides the necessary means for denying to husbands an unequal position in relation to their wives, thus discarding the traditional view of headship-submission. The very fear that headship implies dominance is enough to incline most feminists to choose this interpretation. And this is altogether understandable to anyone aware of the history of male dominance.

The question, however, goes much deeper than the manifestation of male dominance and its unacceptability. The real question concerns a correct biblical theology of headship and our willing obedience to it. So let's first seek to determine the biblical meaning and significance of the term.

The theological vocabulary of early Christian writings in Greek, beginning with the subapostolic age and embracing the era of the creeds and councils on down to the Second Council of Nicea in 787, is interpreted in *A Patristic Greek Lexicon*. It is indicated therein that many writers used the term *head*. Sometimes the meaning is *preeminence* and *authority of position*, sometimes *origin*, or *source of being*. Thus both usages were established very early. But, predominantly, when Christ is represented as Head of the church, it is His authority and preeminence that are generally in mind.

There are two passages that incline interpreters toward the meaning of *origin*, or *source of being*. First is Ephesians 4:15, 16. Here the key words are, "we are to grow up in every way into him who is the head, into Christ, from whom the whole body, joined and knit together by every joint with which it is supplied, when each part is working properly, makes bodily growth and upbuilds itself in love." The second passage is Colossians 2:19, "the Head, from whom the whole body, nourished and knit together through its joints and ligaments, grows with a growth that is from God." Notice the similarity of the two passages, and the thought that the head is that which gives growth to the body.

Richard Batey, in a major study, says that Paul, influenced by the Septuagint Version, uses *kephale* (head) to refer to *authority grounded in priority of being*. Batey says, "In a patriarchal social structure where leadership depended on seniority, or priority of being, the association of 'first' with 'leadership' was instinctive."[1] He further notes, "Since the church originally derived her being from Christ, she is ontically dependent upon him."[2] Thus, as the source of the church's being, the *precedence* of Christ becomes linked with His *preeminence*. His position as the first-born means that He occupies a determinative and dominant place. Herman Ridderbos points out that Jewish thought considered one who was a progenitor to have inherent status as leader.

1. Richard A. Batey, *New Testament Nuptial Imagery* (Leiden: E. J. Brill, 1971), p. 24.
2. Ibid., p. 25.

Paul repeatedly uses *head* in a metaphorical sense with no thought of a body belonging to it; hence there is no sense of its being a source. To illustrate, in I Corinthians 11:3 God is said to be the Head of Christ; does this mean that Christ is God's body? Christ Himself is said to be the Head of every man; does this imply that every man comprises Christ's body? In Ephesians 1:22 Christ is termed the Head over all things, while in Colossians 2:10 He is the Head over all principality and power (KJV). Does this mean that the "all things" and "all principality and power" are His body? In these instances, headship has nothing to do with source of being, but altogether with preeminence, authority, and rule.

The further we go, the more we are convinced that *kephale* (head) as *source of being, origin,* or *beginning,* is purely secondary to Paul's thought, a precondition to preeminence. Christ's position of authority and rule is grounded in His priority of being. In confirmation, one need only review the more extended passages, Ephesians 1:20–22 and Colossians 1:15–18.

In Ephesians 1:20–22 we read that God

> raised [Christ] from the dead and made him sit at his right hand in the heavenly places, far above all rule and authority and power and dominion, and above every name that is named, not only in this age but also in that which is to come; and he has put all things under his feet and has made him the head over all things for the church.

What ideas go together with headship? "Far above all rule . . . authority . . . power . . . dominion . . . above every name . . . all things under his feet . . . has made him the head over all things for the church." Here is a picture of highest preeminence, of one who is worthy of all authority and power, who as victor over sin and death is henceforth made Head over all things for the church. Christ has won the highest position—headship, given Him by the Father.

Or take Colossians 1:15–18:

He is the image of the invisible God, the first-born of all creation; for in him all things were created, in heaven and on earth, visible and invisible, whether thrones or dominions or principalities or authorities—all things were created through him and for him. He is before all things, and in him all things hold together. He is the head of the body, the church; he is the beginning, the first-born from the dead, that in everything he might be pre-eminent.

Both meanings of headship are intimately combined in this passage. The sense of source of being could not be clearer. Christ is referred to as the first-born of all creation, the beginning, before all things, in whom all things hold together. All things were created for Him. But is this the sum and substance of it? By no means! There is a consummate end to which all of this tends, and apart from which all is meaningless: "that in everything he might be pre-eminent." In other words, the climax which these preconditions make possible is His preeminent position! Karl Barth caught this precisely, defining headship in terms of "the superior, the first, the leader, the bearer of primary responsibility."

This progress of thought, from Christ the Head *as the source of life and being for the church,* to *His preeminence and authority,* is further clarified in Colossians 2:9, 10, "For in him the whole fulness of deity dwells bodily, and you have come to fulness of life in him, who is the head of all rule and authority." Prominent once again is the thought that the church derives her life from Jesus. When He is mentioned as Head, however, notice how the figure changes to emphasize that He is the "head of all rule and authority." This confirms what we find stated in the Arndt-Gingrich lexicon, that in the case of living beings, the figurative use of *kephale* (head) "denotes superior rank." As a case in point, Ephesians 5:23 is cited.

Heinrich Schlier, writing in the *Theological Dictionary of the New Testament,* indicates that the Septuagint Version, the Greek translation of the Old Testament which was in use before the Christian era, used the word *head* to represent what is superior, or determinative. In New Testament usage, the word "implies one who stands over another in the sense of being the ground of his being."[3] So, to have prior being, and to be the source of another's being, entitles one to stand above another with respect to position and authority.

Perhaps we gain a more adequate idea of our relationship to Christ as our exalted Head when we see ourselves in the worship imagery of Revelation 5:12, 13:

> "Worthy is the Lamb that hath been slain to receive the power, and riches, and wisdom, and might, and honor, and glory, and blessing." And every created thing which is in the heaven, and on the earth, and under the earth, and on the sea, and all things that are in them, heard I saying, "Unto him that sitteth on the throne, and unto the Lamb, *be* the blessing, and the honor, and the glory, and the dominion, for ever and ever." (ASV)

To diminish the headship of Christ to nothing more than *source of being,* or *beginning,* and then attempt to make that a sufficient model for the headship of husbands, is to miss entirely the significance of the position of both. Not that we are pressing for the undue glorification of husbands! But God's Word certainly has something more than source of being in view when it speaks of headship.

In this magnificent passage from Revelation, the exalted Lamb of God is not even referred to in terms of His being the *Beginning,* or the *Source of being.* Rather, the emphasis is on what the crucified and risen Christ has acquired: "power . . . riches . . . wisdom . . . might . . . honor . . . glory . . . blessing . . . dominion." We see our exalted Head in His position of preeminence. If we are to understand the headship of the husband as modeled on the headship of Christ, then let us see His headship in the fulness of its majesty, in the fulness of the headship which

---

3. *Theological Dictionary of the New Testament,* ed. Gerhard Kittel, ed. and trans. G. W. Bromiley (Grand Rapids: Eerdmans, 1965), vol. 3, p. 679.

Scripture ascribes to Him. Then let us see in what ways God commands husbands to emulate that headship.

Headship in Relation to Subjection

In Scripture the concept of the headship of husbands is found in connection with the concept of the subjection of wives. The primary meaning of the word translated *subjection,* or *submission,* is "the state of being placed under someone or something." Is one placed under a "source" or an "authority"? The use of these two terms together makes the answer rather obvious. Moreover, wives are commanded to be subject to their husbands in "all things" (Eph. 5:24), calling to mind Christ's being made "head over all things for the church" (Eph. 1:22). The force of the parallel use of "all things" in the two passages confirms the understanding of headship as a position of preeminence, of status or rank, and implying authority and responsibility.

Does this not most likely explain why Paul, in view of his call, "Be subject to one another" (Eph. 5:21), does not say, "Wives, be subject to your husbands, *and husbands, be subject to your wives"*? The simple reason why he doesn't *say* that is that he doesn't *mean* that! Headship and submission in marriage are not reversible. Nor are they rescindable.

Granted, there are obvious differences between the headship of Christ over the church, and the headship of the husband over the wife. Both the similarities and the dissimilarities can be ascertained from Ephesians 5:21–33. These differences, however, do not in any way diminish the analogy; rather, they serve to clarify the characteristics and distinctiveness belonging to each.

We should be reminded that the passage under discussion, Ephesians 5:21–33, belongs to a larger context which extends to 6:9, and includes two other social relationships besides marriage—that of parents to children, and masters to slaves. Interestingly, in none of these relationships does Paul elaborate a theme of mutual subjection. Rather, he proceeds to the particulars of each relational structure, showing that there are given roles in each case, roles which call for a distinct form of authority and the proper subjection to it. Each instance illustrates how Christians are to be "subject to one another" within prescribed roles, not equally subject to one another.

Theodore Wedel, writing in the *Interpreter's Bible*, aptly sorts out these details:

> The head of the household, whether in his capacity of husband, father, or master of slaves, cannot be subject to his wife, his children, and his slaves, as they to him. Yet he cannot wield authority as a self-asserting tyrant. He is entrusted with a responsibility by One who shows the way for its execution; toward his wife, self-sacrificing love; toward his children, to care for their nurture in the things of the Spirit; toward his slaves, a reciprocity of good will. His whole demeanor is to be determined by the constant recollection that he himself is a slave to Christ. He is to be the kind of authority, or head, to others that Christ is to him.[4]

In not one of the three relationships is Paul talking about anything other than the structure of authority and the proper subjection to it. The first of the three, marriage, is no exception.

We should note that whereas headship connotes preeminence, authority, and responsibility, it does not define the specific means by which preeminence, authority, and responsibility are to function. Rather, this is determined by the special nature of each given relationship, and by whatever conditions are placed upon it by the decree of God for whose purpose the relationship exists.

While the headship of husbands is strictly a New Testament concept, fully drawn by the apostle Paul, it is hinted at, if not explicitly taught, in creation. In contrast to many writers today who stress Genesis 1, while either ignoring Genesis 2 or placing

---

4. Theodore O. Wedel, "Ephesians," in *Interpreter's Bible*, ed. George A. Buttrick (New York: Abingdon, 1953), vol. 10, p. 718.

it in contradiction to Genesis 1, Paul Jewett makes this reasonable observation:

> While the first creation narrative, which includes the fundamental affirmation that man in the divine image is male and female (Gen. 1:27), contains no hint of such a hierarchical view, the second narrative (Gen. 2:18–23), which we have treated as supplementing the first, allows, if it does not actually imply, that the woman is subordinate to the man. Here we are told that the woman was created *from* and *for* man.[5]

In this connection we observe an interesting correlation: just as Jesus appealed to creation (explicitly Gen. 2:24) to teach God's will for permanence in marriage (see, e.g., Matt. 19:5), so Paul also appeals to creation (again, Gen. 2:24) to teach God's will for the permanence of the headship-submission relation in marriage. It should be observed that immediately at the close of his main exposition of headship-submission (Eph. 5:22–30), he quotes Genesis 2:24, saying, "For this reason." Can we fail to recognize that the marriage relationship under the order of headship-submission, with its genius for harmonious fulfillment rooted in the husband's Christlike, self-sacrificing love, is the very reason in God's plan why "a man shall leave his father and mother and be joined to his wife, and the two shall become one" (Eph. 5:31)? Each part of the divine equation is necessary to every other part. One must ask why it is that some today are so anxious to minimize these clear scriptural truths.

I think we know why this is so. Historically, men have greatly misunderstood and abused the idea of headship. They have simplistically assumed that it means that they are the boss, and any kind of boss they please to be, turning headship into a self-aggrandizing position of domination over their wives. But while we share the desire to eradicate all traces of this kind of

---

5. Paul K. Jewett, *Man as Male and Female* (Grand Rapids: Eerdmans, 1975), p. 50.

false assumption, and the behavior it creates, the first question is: Does the solution lie in the rejection of the biblically established concept of husband-headship? Or does it lie in a right understanding of what God intends and in instructing Christian couples how God's intention might be appropriately fulfilled? Obviously, our prime task is to enable husbands to conform to the biblical ideal.

Headship invests the husband with one more reason to be in subjection to Christ, his Head. Now he must function in a similar capacity toward his wife; he cannot do this on his own. In fact, he will carry out this function only in selfish, inadequate, even abusive ways if he himself is not in subjection to the Lord.

A question properly raised at this point is whether the wife, if she is under the headship of her husband, is then not directly under the headship of Christ. Is the husband the only spouse in that relationship to Christ? This would be a serious inference to draw, for all Christians—including wives—are under the headship of Christ in a primary way. Nevertheless, it is equally true, and not at all incompatible, that in a secondary way a woman as wife is under the special headship of her husband.

It is only as a husband's authority over his wife grows out of his own subjection to Christ, and only as he is accountable to Him, that his headship can function authentically. For when a husband lives under the lordship of Christ, then he can be trusted with the authority, responsibility, and governance which God commands. It cannot be otherwise.

Headship in Practice

We understand what headship for husbands means in *positional* terms; what does it mean in *practical* terms? We can accept the divine order laid down in heaven; can we accept the way the order works out on earth as well? What can wives really expect? In what way is a husband to take precedence? Karl Barth suggests:

> Certainly not in order to be something more and greater and
> other than she! Certainly not to his own advantage and her dis-
> advantage. But for her sake, that she might follow him! And
> where does this course lead her? Not into an unworthy and irk-
> some dependence on him, but into her own characteristic free-
> dom in relation to him! He is her head in the fact that he sum-
> mons her to this goal, i.e., that he makes himself primarily re-
> sponsible for their common advance toward it, to freedom and
> fellowship.[6]

Thus, headship is not at all a husband's becoming a master,
boss, tyrant, authoritarian—the dominant, coercive force.
Neither does it imply control or restriction, his being assertive
and her being suppressed. It cannot mean he assumes any pre-
rogatives of greater virtue, intelligence, or ability. It does not
mean that he is active and she passive, he the voice and she the
silent partner. Nor does it mean that he is the tribal chief, the
family manager, the one who has superior rights or privileges.
He is not the decision-maker, problem-solver, goal-setter, or
director of everyone else in the family's life. Rather, he is, as
Barth says, primarily responsible for their common advance toward freedom and fellowship—creating a partnership of equals
under one responsible head.

Husbands may not rule on their own behalf or by their own
authority—certainly not by their own selfish whim! Nor can
there be anything arbitrary about their exercise of headship; it
must derive from the headship of Christ in the husband's own
life. In no sense does his headship originate in his own will and
desire. He does not lord it over his wife and thus stifle her
growth as a person or partner. Headship is not so much a
privilege as a responsibility, and it is for this reason that the
greater burden by far is placed upon husbands. The privilege
lies in fulfilling love's highest objectives. Headship "over" one's
wife is transformed by love into headship "on behalf of" her

---

6. Karl Barth, *Church Dogmatics* III/1, tr. J. W. Edwards, O. Bussey, and Harold
   Knight (Edinburgh: T. & T. Clark, 1961), pp. 301ff.

welfare and growth. Headship under the model of Ephesians 5:25–31 finds its complete essence, as we shall see, in Christlike, self-giving love.

In keeping with the nature of Christian headship, husbands are never told that they are to make their wives subject to themselves. Love takes great initiative, but never in a coercive way. Interestingly, the verb form for subjection is almost exclusively in the middle or passive voice in New Testament Greek, indicating it is *someone subjecting himself to another,* not someone subjecting another to himself. It is the wife who in obedience to Christ subjects herself to her husband, doing so as a natural consequence of her freedom in Christ and her desire to do His will.

The Love That Makes It All Work

The single command to husbands, the only defining word as to how their headship is to express itself, is found in verse 25: "Husbands, love your wives, as Christ loved the church and gave himself up for her." The whole plan of God is encompassed in this single imperative.

German theologian Helmut Thielicke states this very important qualification of headship: the husband is superior, but not superior in a sociological sense; he is superior in the sense of his imitation of Christ.[7] The headship of the male is to be a primacy within a relation where two stand equally under the grace of God, a primacy determined by love and the willingness to serve.

Note how great is the special command laid upon husbands —greater it would seem than that laid upon wives. In fact, the demand upon husbands is calculated to alleviate altogether the burden which subjection might otherwise lay upon wives. This is the genius of God's mandate for those with spiritual wisdom to understand it. What the wife is subject to is not

7. Helmut Thielicke, *The Ethics of Sex,* tr. John W. Doberstein (New York: Harper & Row, 1964), pp. 11–13.

some arbitrary, self-willed authority figure; *she is subject to self-giving love.*

Headship demands the rule of *agape*-love, no less. What is this, but an extraordinary, more-than-human love, a love of which Jesus Christ is the sole model? The specifics are outlined in I Corinthians 13. Truly, only the indwelling Spirit of God can enable a husband to reach out in this kind of love! But when he seeks to do this, how beautiful it is! How privileged the wife who in consequence of her subjection to her husband finds that the dominant thrust of his headship over her is the rule of *agape*-love!

As the church finds her delight in subjecting herself to the loving headship of her Lord, so the wife can find her delight in subjecting herself to the loving headship of an earnest Christian husband who is genuinely trying to model his love for her after the pattern of Christ's love for the church. Granted, this is an incredible ideal, but not impossible of growing fulfillment. We must not discard ideals because they appear too high!

At the very heart of true love is a reaching out to affirm and enhance the beloved. As Harry Overstreet puts it, it is the love, not of *possession*, but of *affirmation*. It is giving without primary concern for compensating reward. Such a love, of course, cannot and will not exploit, intimidate, manipulate, or control. Nor can it suppress whatever is truly just and good for the beloved. Any wife would be safe, secure, and satisfied under the protecting shield of such love.

I can hear some wife whisper to herself at this point, "But this does not describe *my* husband." And I can hear some husband whisper to himself, "But this does not describe *my* wife." The real problem, as I see it, is not the structure of headship-submission, but rather the implementation of it. It is failure on the part of one or both of the spouses that keeps it from being the beautiful thing God means it to be. In marriage workshops all over the nation, couples are realistically facing up to their past ignorance of God's design, or their unwillingness to fulfill their roles in obedience to Christ.

The demands of *agape*-love are not easy to face, to be sure. For husbands, it may mean relinquishing some tightly scheduled time to afford adequate allowance for his marriage to develop. Or it may mean spending less time with old buddies or special interests such as sports, TV, or hobbies. It could mean lessening some career ambitions. Whatever the cost, a Christian husband in obedience to the Lord will allow nothing to take priority over commitment to his wife. At the very least, it will require a listening ear, an understanding heart, an empathic spirit, and the initiative toward service.

The essence of God's command to husbands is further elucidated in verse 28: "Even so husbands should love their wives as their own bodies." This imperative is pursued for five more verses, under the reasoning that no man hates his own flesh, but nourishes and cherishes it. In the intimacy of marriage, where two spouses consider themselves "one flesh" in the Lord, a husband should find it the most natural thing in the world to treat his wife as his own body, seeing to her every care. With something so dearly a part of himself, is there any place for neglect or abuse? *Christian husbands don't stand on authority; they stoop in love!*

A loving husband will always defer to his wife—her desires, her tastes, her opinions, her participation in a decision—in every facet of life together. Love will make him facilitate his wife's growth and development. That same love will restrain and correct any temptation to use his authority to her disadvantage and to his own advantage. The love of Christ is the great corrective for all the ways in which a man needs to improve his living relationship with his wife.

But there is a danger lest we so emphasize the model of Christ's unconditional love that we fail to see human love as fragile, often failing, and in need of being returned. At best we can only approximate the love of Christ in its altruism. We need to be loved in return, accepted, and affirmed as well. Our human love *is* human. Larry Christenson caught this very nicely in his suggestion that if a husband says, "I will love my wife for her own sake, asking nothing in return," he may be simply patronizing, taking a superior place, and in the process becoming a cold, distant, and detached individual. This, of course, is not love by any definition! Christenson's comment is apropos:

> The Bible is at once more profound and more practical. It sees a husband's love for his wife springing not from disinterested altruism, but from a profound personal unity. . . . He cannot take care of himself without at the same time taking care of his body, for he and his body are one.[8]

The incredible thing about Jesus is that He never once manipulated any person for any purpose. He refused to lead from strength, and instead led from a loving sensitivity to others' special needs. Hence He was always vulnerable. How incomprehensible this must be to our self-actualizing and self-fulfilling society! Yet what real strength this takes—strength of purpose, of self-denial, of discipline—strength to lead from love! Jesus expressed it when He said, "He who loses his life for my sake will find it" (Matt. 10:39b). Love, then, has a logic of its own—the logic of headship-submission as delineated in Ephesians 5!

The Ends Served by Headship

The *manner* in which headship fulfills itself is *love;* what are the *ends* which it is to fulfill? Three thoughts are brought out in verses 26, 27: "that he [Christ] might sanctify her [the church] . . . that he might present the church to himself in splendor . . . that she might be holy and without blemish." Curiously, Paul mentions nothing about what Christ Himself shall gain from the exercise of His headship. That He Himself receives in return is perfectly true. But the emphasis, you see, is only upon what His bride, the church, shall receive. Similarly, we are to

---

8. Larry Christenson, *The Christian Couple* (Minneapolis: Bethany Fellowship, 1977), p. 35.

understand that the end purpose of a loving husband's commitment to his wife is that she will be truly actualized to the full extent of her own growth potential.

This picture of Christ presenting His bride to Himself has its roots in Jewish wedding customs. The presentation of the bride to the bridegroom was entrusted to the "friend of the bride." The bride's best man, as it were, functioned much as the bride's father does today. But in Ephesians it would be especially noticeable to Jewish Christians that here it is not a friend of the bride, but Christ Himself who presents the bride to Himself. Is this not just one more suggestion of what the headship of Christ entails, and how husbands are to model after it? Each husband has the responsibility, and each takes the initiative, to present his bride in perfection at last. This is the continuing work of our heavenly Head; it is also the model for every Christian husband.

A truly loving husband will regard his wife as a completely equal partner in everything that concerns their life together. He will assert his headship to see that this equal partnership is kept inviolable. Hers is to be an equal contribution in areas, say, of decision-making, conflict-resolution, emerging family developmental planning, and daily family management. Whether it concerns finances, or child discipline, or social life—whatever it may be, she is an equal partner. Loving headship affirms, defers, shares; it encourages and stimulates. Loving headship delights to delegate without demanding. Yet, throughout the equalitarian process, the husband knows all the while that he bears responsibility before God for the healthful maintenance of the marriage.

The practical truth is that the husband is charged with the responsibility of leadership, but not with providing all the answers, directions, and implementations. He is responsible to see that decisions get made, not that he as an authoritarian make them on his own. He is responsible to see that problems and conflicts are resolved, not that he himself independently come up with and impose those solutions. He is to see that the relationship stays healthy and grows as it should, especially in spiritual ways, but not according to his independent or arbitrary initiative. He is to use his headship position to see that the marriage functions properly and brings satisfactions in equal shares to both partners.

One consequence of the husband's ultimate headship responsibility requires a comment. It concerns the failure of two people to come to a common decision. Should there be an occasion where a critical decision must be made, when a couple have rationally and prayerfully explored every possibility, yet fail to reach agreement, what then? Only then must the husband make the decision. He must make it within the context of his loving concern and with the realization that he is taking responsibility for the outcome, for the way it will affect them both. While he is accountable to God because of his headship, he is also answerable to his wife as well. Such decisions, as any husband knows who has had to make one, are hardly to be considered "the husband's privilege." These are solemn, often lonely and painful moments. A wife may be grateful indeed not to be charged with such ultimate responsibility. And while this appears to be the course to follow in such an instance, it should be a rare occasion indeed, perhaps one that in many marriages is never necessary.

Jesus and Wives as Servants

If the husband is the head of the wife as Christ is the Head of the church, and if the wife represents the church, does this imply that the wife is not representative of Christ in any way?

Jesus Christ is not only the *Head* (represented by husbands), but the *Servant* also (represented by wives). Both headship and servanthood belong to the majesty and glory of Christ our Lord. He, you see, is also the sum of all subjection and servanthood. Philippians 2:6, 7 affirms this: "who, though he was in the form of God, did not count equality with God a thing to be grasped, but emptied himself, taking the form of a servant." He gladly exchanged equality with God for servanthood! He Himself said to His disciples, "He who is greatest among you shall be your servant" (Matt. 23:11), and "The Son of man came not to be ministered unto, but to minister" (Mark 10:45, KJV). The very essence of His life was that of ministering servant. The *Head* is the *Servant!*

Might we say, by implication, that wives have equality, too; yet after the model of Jesus, they are not to count equality a thing to be grasped, but are to take on the form of a servant in subjection to their husbands. Is it too much that the Servant Christ should ask this of wives?

To such servanthood every Christian is called, both men and women, husbands and wives. It is to special subjection that the Christian wife is called. But since love is the essence of servanthood, we come full circle and see the undeniable fact that husbands are called to the very same thing! In a special sense, they can learn from their wives what is the nature of their own servanthood.

Back to the question which prompted these thoughts. Yes, the wife is representative of Christ—*Christ the Servant*. She models this majestic feature of our Lord's person as truly as husbands model His leadership.

To conclude this chapter, let us be reminded once more of the incredible fact that God regards Christian marriage as representative of the union between Christ and the church. What can we say of that union but that it is founded on self-giving love, continued in faithfulness, and expressed through the deepest possible commitment to caring? This being the model, should any Christian couple find reason to want to rescind God's gracious order for their marriage? If by God's grace they find enablement to fulfill their respective roles, can they not trust Him to bless their obedience? Will not the great Head of the church, even Jesus Himself, bring about an incomparable harmony and oneness of spirit? Will He not satisfy the hearts of both partners, granting them happiness and fulfillment in equal shares?

To be obedient to God's order requires a deeper commitment

still—subjection of all of life to the lordship of Jesus Christ. On this deeper level the real test takes place. Submission to the Lord is the way of peace and joy in every relationship on earth. Headship in the love of Jesus is a beautiful thing; subjection in the love of Jesus is an equally beautiful thing. Confidently we can say that neither spouse need resent God's appointed role. *Life in partnership under God's rule is best!*

It should be clear by now that the rationale for equal-partnership marriage is biblically valid, but is not to be found in Ephesians 5:21. Further on I shall show that it cannot be established on the basis of Galatians 3:28 either, as so many insist. Yet, no less than others, I contend for equally shared roles in marriage! Our argument finds its support, not in the structure of marriage, but in its unique manner of functioning. Husbands and wives mutually interact out of Christlike, self-giving love, which husbands translate into the subjection of a caring, serving self, and which wives translate into loving servanthood.

As was pointed out at the end of chapter 1, the starting point for the husband is headship, for the wife subjection. But the common end-result finds each in loving subjection to the other. Each renders the same ministry to the other, a ministry destined to bring harmony and happiness in equal shares.

The paradox which is difficult for the secular mind to comprehend is simply this: Husbands and wives are different but equal; they are equal but different. They share equal personhood, equal status, equal place, equal expression of gifts, equal spiritual standing, equal individual autonomy. They are equal in everything but in the divinely appointed headship of authority and responsibility granted to husbands. The husband is given the responsibility and its commensurate authority to see that the marriage is and becomes what God designs it to be. This includes seeing that the wife is an equal participant in everything that concerns the marriage.

Have you been hung up on headship? soured on submission? As we let Scripture state its own message, the concepts of headship and submission begin to make sense. Do not the culturally distorted images of headship and submission begin to fall away beside the divine paradox? Thomas Howard gives an apt summary in a recent article in *Christianity Today:*

> With respect to my wife, I am instructed by the Apostle to be "head." Not boss; head. The Apostle gives me my cue here by referring to the headship of the divine bridegroom vis-à-vis his spouse. It is a headship brought as gift, not wielded as club, and offered—"submitted," if you will—*to* her, *for* her, in obedience to the divine choreography, so to speak. I did not think it up.
>
> What is this headship, if it is not boss-hood? Here again, I must take my cues from the Apostle, nay from the Lord himself: it seems to have something to do with answerability before God. Somehow I am the one who stands before the most high as the one responsible for this family. Responsible all by myself? Surely not, since I am made one with my spouse here. And yet, just as the one, single act of procreation distributed itself between the two of us for one single end, so here there is no question of exchanging roles, any more than there is of Christ, in the interest of his spouse's health and freedom, stepping aside and saying, "Right. Now we adopt the round-table model." What can it mean? I am not sure *what* it means, any more than I can unscramble and plot out the mystery of the Eucharist. But I obey, and in obeying, move perhaps slowly but nonetheless farther and farther, towards the place where I will be vouchsafed to see what it all means.[9]

Before the mystery of God's design, the response is simply that—*obedience!* It is not ours to question God's appointment, much less to discard it as—in our eyes—culturally passé. May we, too, in obeying, move towards the place where we shall see what it all means.

In the words of Robert Farrar Capon, "[The husband] *is* the head. He will be a good one or a bad one, depending; but if he isn't the head, there isn't any other."[10]

---

9. Thomas Howard, "The Yoke of Fatherhood," *Christianity Today,* 23 June 1978, p. 13.
10. Robert Farrar Capon, *Bed and Board: Plain Talk About Marriage* (New York: Simon and Schuster, 1965), p. 54.

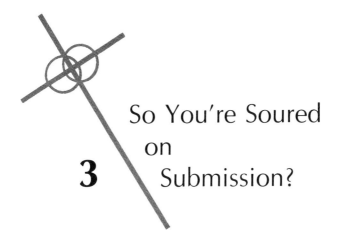

So You're Soured on Submission?

3

In our descriptive analysis of the headship of the Christian husband, we noted the scriptural correspondence between the husband's headship and the wife's subjection. The present chapter is designed to bring together some additional thoughts on subjection, both to clarify and expand our understanding. But first, a brief review may serve to sharpen what will be presented in the pages ahead.

We noted that the primary meaning of the Greek word for subjection is "the state of being placed under someone or something." In Paul's Epistles, it is used mostly in the sense of placing oneself under the authority of another—servants under masters, the church under its leadership, Christians under those who rule over them governmentally.

We stated that the primary meaning of headship in its New Testament usage is "authority." This corresponds most closely with the meaning "the state of being placed under someone or something," as we understand the definition of subjection. We know precisely what each of these two words—headship and subjection—signifies when placed in relation to one another. To be subject to headship is to be under authority. Thus, in New Testament terms, we cannot separate either headship or subjection from the order of authority which God has appointed for marriage.

What Subjection Does Not Mean

In previous comments we suggested that subjection has long been misunderstood and misapplied in marriage. It is necessary, therefore, to emphasize from the start just what subjection is not.

Since headship does not mean a domineering husband, or one who assumes an authoritarian position, subjection does not mean a passive response to some dominant form of authoritarianism. Nor does headship stand for coercion, control, manipulation, or the imposition of one's will upon another. Of one thing we can be sure: subjection does not make a wife fair game for a husband's arbitrary exercise of will.

Because headship does not imply superior rights or privileges, subjection cannot imply inferior rights or privileges. Nor can we equate headship with the active marital role, subjection with the passive role. And inasmuch as headship has nothing to do with superior intellect, insight, virtue, or ability, so also we may assume that wifely subjection is not inferiority in any of these respects.

The husband may very well hold the position of headship, yet Scripture contains no suggestion that he occupies an elevated status while his wife occupies a lower one. It is quite impermissible to think that because the roles of husband and wife differ significantly, one is more important than the other. If headship is to function as self-giving, Christlike love, then subjection must function as giving precedence to this extension of Christ's love. To do otherwise would be to shut off His love. Love, you see, is thus the controlling factor, a husband's love making a wife's subjection completely acceptable to her, even desirable.

We should make no mistake about this: although husbands are commanded to love their wives, wives are not called to subject themselves to love, but to headship. God doesn't say, "Wives, be subject to your husbands when they are loving," any more than He says, "Husbands, love your wives when they are in subjection to you." The command in each instance is an unconditional imperative which in no way is dependent upon what the other does or does not do.

Extending this line of thought, we can appreciate the fact that subjection is never conceptualized in terms of servitude or passive submission. A wife is to contribute to the relationship. She is not to be left out of major decision-making and day-by-day family management. Can headship-subjection mean anything less than equal contribution to every facet of married life? In no way is a wife's spirit to be suppressed, or her will put down by a husband's stronger will. Any form of subjection which results in any demeaning of the wife whatever cannot be of God.

It should go without saying that subjection is not silence. Nowhere is it the intent of Scripture that a wife subject herself to thoughtlessness or to harsh insensitivity. Of course, she may choose, for the Lord's sake, to endure a wrong done to her. Depending upon the situation and likely consequences, this may or may not be wise. But she is not denied recourse to corrective means. There are specific biblical principles for redressing wrongs. Accusation and nagging, however, are not among them! But it is always proper to seek what is right. Only it must be done in a right spirit, a subject spirit.

A truly subject wife will be aware of those times when she is tempted to move out of her role and become demanding, aggressive, perhaps resentful and bitter. Here we may legitimately apply the word in I Peter 3:1, "Likewise you wives, be submissive to your husbands, so that some, though they do not obey the word, may be won without a word by the behavior of their wives." Commentators generally assume that Peter is referring to Christian wives married to pagan husbands, and that the best witness to such husbands is through behavior, not "preaching." But this is not explicit in the language. It may very well refer to a Christian husband who nevertheless is disobedient to God's Word as it concerns his relationship to his wife. A subject wife, by her behavior, may then win the heart of the recalcitrant husband, causing him to love her as he ought, and to treat her in ways consonant with Christ's love.

We must be clear about this: we cannot ever say that women are by nature subject creatures. This is the mistake of Judith Miles. Writing in *The Feminine Principle: A Woman's Discovery of the Key to Total Fulfillment*, she reasons that women are "incarnate models of submission and loyalty."[1] If this were so, there would not be the massive uprising in our day against the biblical doctrine. No, it has nothing to do with nature. There is no such thing as a "subject type" of personality, feminine or otherwise. This is the worst kind of stereotyping! Subjection has to do only with God's command to Christian wives.

What Subjection Does Mean

We've probably devoted more attention than is warranted to what subjection is not. Yet it is important that there be no false notions as to the nature of this special calling. The long history of its abuse is reason enough to clarify the matter as fully as possible. Wives understandably bristle at the very thought of what suggests to their minds a most inequitable arrangement. Traditional stereotypes of headship-subjection are badly in need of correction, all will quickly admit. In a more positive sense we need to see the beauty and power of subjection as one of our Lord's chief virtues, mutual subjection as a way of life for every Christian, and subjection to their husbands as God's special vocation for Christian wives.

---

1. Judith Miles, *The Feminine Principle: A Woman's Discovery of the Key to Total Fulfillment* (St. Louis: Bethany Press, 1975), p. 51.

There seems to be much confusion as to the exact meaning of subjection, as used in the New Testament. The Revised Standard Version employs three English terms to translate the Greek word. However, only two of them are used when the reference is to marriage. Those two are "subjection" and "submission." The third word, "subordination," is found in other contexts, but never in reference to marriage.

Harvard professor Helmut Köster, writing in the *Theological Dictionary of the New Testament*, says of the Greek word for subjection: "Originally it is a hierarchical term which stresses the relation to superiors."[2] In relation to the subjection of a wife to her husband, "the issue is keeping a divinely willed order."[3] Again, he refers to subjection as "a term of order" (which is precisely what lexicons say about the term *headship* as well). Köster also says that "the general rule demands readiness to renounce one's own will for the sake of others . . . and to give precedence to others."[4] So quite evidently *subjection is one's response to a person holding a superior position of authority.*

It is the observation of Marcus Barth that in all cases where the New Testament uses the term, a hierarchy is present. He notes, too, that in Paul's usage it always describes a voluntary attitude of giving and of cooperating. The verb form of "subjection" is almost exclusively found in the middle or passive voice in Greek, the import of this being that *one subjects himself to another,* he is not subjected by another.

We gain the immediate impression that a wife's subjection is meant to be a willing response to God's personal call. It is her desire, arising out of her freedom in Christ, out of her new sense of spiritual values in personal relationships, and, most importantly, out of her obedient subjection to Christ first of all. It is but one part of her total response to His lordship in her life. Never coerced, it is no less than the power of Christ's own subjection working in her by the Holy Spirit.

---

2. *Theological Dictionary of the New Testament*, ed. Gerhard Kittel, ed. and trans. G. W. Bromiley (Grand Rapids: Eerdmans, 1965), vol. 13, p. 45.
3. Ibid.
4. Ibid.

Karl Olsson comments: "A woman in Christ is no longer an enslaved but a free spirit who accepts the necessities of existence with grace, and by a curious paradox the subjection thus accepted ceases to be just subjection and becomes an opportunity for free and loving service."[5] Yes, subjection is transformed by grace in the same way that headship is transformed by grace.

We should be reminded that authentic humanity is servanthood. As creatures of the fall we've forgotten this. But servanthood is appropriate to the purpose for which we were created, since in serving God's creatures we are serving Him. Such service acknowledges the dignity of our humanity, for what is higher in us than service freely rendered from a will surrendered to God? Yet at the fall this quality of authentic humanity was perverted, turned into self-serving. But with redemption, our service is turned inside out, as it were. Once again it is possible to fulfill our humanity through serving others. Martin Luther captured the paradox of the Christian life in these words: "A Christian is the most free lord of all and subject to none; a Christian is the most dutiful servant of all and subject to everyone."[6]

In no way is God's plan for subjection—whether as the Christian's lifestyle, or the special vocation of Christian wives—a violation of our humanity. It is its highest fulfillment. Within marriage, there is no more excellent way in which a man and woman together can fulfill their partnership under God, experiencing at the same time the "one flesh" relationship.

Paul's command in Ephesians 5:22 is, "Wives, be subject to your husbands, as to the Lord." In verse 24 we read, "As the church is subject to Christ, so let wives also be subject in everything to their husbands." Subjection is qualified by the words "as to the Lord" and "in everything."

What does Paul mean by "as to the Lord"? Surely not that *the*

---

5. Karl Olsson, *Seven Sins and Seven Virtues* (New York: Harper & Row, 1962), p. 61.
6. Quoted in Elaine Stedman, *A Woman's Worth* (Waco, TX: Word Books, 1975), p. 58.

husband is the lord of the wife! And most certainly not *"to the same extent* that you are subject to the Lord." It quite possibly means, *"in the same manner* as you are subject to the Lord," but most likely, *"as a part of your subjection to the Lord."* At any rate, we understand a wife's subjection to her husband is to be modeled after her subjection to Christ—as a part of her obedience to His command. She is willing, in other words, to be subject to her husband because she is subject to the Lord in everything He commands of her.

Do we not now see subjection as the realization of a beautiful quality of the Christian life—the quality of selfless caring? Is there anything more beautifully characteristic of our Lord than this? Here is a virtue which contains such elements as humility, deference, and forbearance, to name but a few. Here is a quality which speaks of maturity, strength, and a deep measure of self-control. It represents the best in self-understanding. A woman who fulfills this calling knows her own worth in Christ. Her security in His perfect will relieves her of all sense of threat. Here is a woman sufficiently advanced spiritually to be able to affirm others without a sense of personal loss. Envy and jealousy have been brought to terms. Such a woman, being inwardly free, will not equate service with servitude. She is free from self-concern, and able to accept, without any contradiction, both the *binding* and *releasing* aspects of marital servanthood.

Subjection in Relation to Respect

At the close of Ephesians 5, in what might be considered a brief but noteworthy summary, wives are told to "respect" their husbands. This raises an immediate question: *What if a wife finds little to respect in her husband's behavior or character?* Since the entire passage has to do with God's design for marital roles, it seems reasonable to assume that what the wife is commanded to respect is her husband's position of headship—*his position, not his person.* Presumably, subjection includes respectful deference to the husband's role, because that role has been appointed by God. Once again, it is evident that whether or not one fulfills his or her marital role is not to be determined by the quality of the spouse's life. Rather, obedience to God's directive is required, regardless of what the other is or does.

In the King James Version, Ephesians 5:33 reads, "Let . . . the wife see that she reverence her husband." I wonder if Marabel Morgan had this verse in mind when she wrote: "It is only when a woman surrenders her life to her husband, reveres and worships him, and is willing to serve him, that she becomes really beautiful to him."[7] That phrase "worships him" is hardly what the word *reverence* or *respect* is intended to convey. One is reminded of the young husband who said, "My wife worships me; she continually brings me burnt offerings!"

Scripture never speaks of a wife's "surrendering her life" to her husband. This interpretation only does harm to the biblical idea of subjection, distorting its very essence. Virginia Mollenkott correctly counters, "It borders on idolatry on one hand, the denial of personhood on the other. It is to God alone that we are to surrender our lives. God alone should be revered and worshipped."[8] The word is "respect" and further identifies the wife's proper attitude toward the role which God has given her husband.

Subjection in Relation to Obedience

Here I must note that Kenneth Taylor does a disservice to our understanding of subjection when, in his free paraphrase, *The Living Bible,* he chooses to substitute "obey" for "be subject" in Ephesians 5:24: "So you wives must willingly obey your hus-

---

7. Marabel Morgan, *The Total Woman* (Old Tappan, NJ: Fleming H. Revell, 1973), p. 80.
8. Virginia Ramey Mollenkott, *Women, Men, and the Bible* (Nashville: Abingdon, 1977), p. 41.

bands." Then, to reinforce his choice of words, he expands on the word *respects* in verse 33, adding the words, "obeying, praising and honoring him."

In the interests of accuracy, we must object to this unwarranted substitution. Marcus Barth and other eminent scholars tell us that the word *subjection* does not in itself incorporate the idea of obedience. What is unfortunate is that the word *obey* inclines us toward the idea that the husband commands, the wife obeys, making for an unequal, one-sided outworking of headship-subjection. This "chain of command" would be difficult to support from the text or context.

Now that all this has been said, let it be noted that some commentators do indeed see obedience as implicit in the term *subjection* and in the concept of a wife's responsiveness to the husband's headship. Commenting on the passage, Ralph Martin says of the apostle Paul, "He is arguing from the Christ-Church relationship to the human marriage tie, not *vice versa*. This is why he 'never tells wives that they are to love their husbands. . . . The reason is that which he gives: Christ loves the Church, but it is for the Church to obey and submit to Christ.' "[9]

While we are diverted at the moment to the word *obey*, a comment on I Peter 3:5, 6 seems in order. The text reads, "So once the holy women who hoped in God used to adorn themselves and were submissive to their husbands, as Sarah obeyed Abraham, calling him lord. And you are now her children if you do right and let nothing terrify you."

It is altogether too easy to read into this more than it says. Peter introduces this material for the sake of illustration. He recalls an Old Testament picture and the absolute obedience of Sarah. But when Peter applies the illustration he is careful not to say that women now are to obey their husbands and call them lord. Not at all. He says that they are Sarah's children if they do

9. Ralph P. Martin, "Ephesians," in *New Bible Commentary*, rev. ed. by Donald Guthrie (Grand Rapids: Eerdmans, 1970), p. 1121. Martin is making use of a quotation from Claude Chavasse's *Bride of Christ* (London: Faber, 1940), p. 77.

right and let nothing terrify them. The obvious change in language is tantamount to saying, "You see, the subjection called for in Christ is nothing to be terrified about. Why, think of Sarah; she was in a position of absolute obedience to Abraham. She even referred to him as 'lord.'" Evidently, this is not asked of Christian wives. What is asked is that they be in subjection to their husbands as to the Lord, as part of their obedience to Him. This is not patriarchalism where the husband is lord, commanding unquestioned obedience. The Old Testament illustration is not meant to apply in every detail, but rather to suggest a comparison which shows the superiority of the command to Christian wives.

Servanthood

For those who have thought deeply on Ephesians 5, a question which we have already considered to some extent in the previous chapter arises again. The husband in his headship is said to represent Christ. The wife represents the church, the inference being that she then does not represent Christ in any way. Is the highest privilege of representing Christ limited entirely to the husband? Only in terms of position, but not in terms of His major attributes of divine personhood. Let's examine this more in detail.

Jesus Christ is not only *Head* but *Servant!* Both headship and servanthood belong to His essential majesty. They are not, however, inherent attributes, but were acquired in the work of redemption. He was *made* Head over all things for the church, says Paul in Ephesians 1:22, and He *took* the form of a servant, according to the same apostle in Philippians 2:7. Although He was appointed Head, He is at the same time the sum of all subjection and servanthood! He is the One who, according to Philippians 2:6, 7, "though he was in the form of God, did not count equality with God a thing to be grasped, but emptied himself, taking the form of a servant."

Equality was something He had, but not something He was unwilling to relinquish. He chose servanthood instead! And thus we are on safe ground when we seek the concrete definition of subjection in the person of the Servant-Lord Himself. He, being free, abased Himself for us. He, being equal with the Father, relinquished that equality to become the Servant for our sakes. Subjection, then, means no less than adopting His way of self-denial for the sake of others.

It is this same Jesus who said, "He who is greatest among you shall be your servant" (Matt. 23:11). His greatness is identified with his servanthood. The wife, in the sense of her unique position of subjection, becomes, in the words of Jesus, "the greatest of all." This is what Karl Barth meant when he wrote that the wife has the greater glory.

Can we forget the words of Jesus, "The Son of man came not to be served but to serve" (Matt. 20:28)? The most notable thing about Jesus is that He gave His life totally as a servant. How truly remarkable that the eternal Son of God had from eternity past full equality with the Father, yet chose to subject Himself to the Father for the work of redemption. There is an enigmatic sense in which His subjection has a permanent character, for Paul declares in I Corinthians 15:28, "When all things are subjected to him, then the Son himself will also be subjected to him who put all things under him, that God may be everything to every one." This is beyond our understanding, but we have at least a glimpse in the earthly subjection of the Son to the Father.

As we've seen, every redeemed person is called to servanthood as the expression of his or her new life in Christ. This is accentuated in Paul's introductory clause to the reference to Jesus' taking the form of a servant: "Have this mind among yourselves . . ." (Phil. 2:5). Servanthood is the identifying mark of every true Christian. But when it comes to marriage, modeling this chief attribute of God's Son is granted to wives, not to husbands. Thus the modeling of the chief attributes of our Lord's glorious personhood is equally distributed to husband and wife alike.

As wives are appointed examples and teachers of subjection, so husbands shall learn something of their own servanthood from these examples. Husbands model the self-giving love of Jesus; wives model the self-giving servanthood of Jesus. How could any insightful Christian spouse want to disavow being a model of his Lord in one of His most glorious attributes?

The Costs and Rewards of Subjection

Our Lord could not have stooped lower before the Father than He did. In so doing He became the epitome of all subjection. But it was not without a sense of ultimate reward. This theme is captured in Hebrews 12:2, "who for the joy that was set before him endured the cross, despising the shame." He had eyes to see beyond the present. Thus His subjection was aimed at securing the highest, most sublime joy. Note the paradox once more: in the greatest giving there is greatest gain. Jesus cannot be accused of taking anything away from wives when He calls them to subjection. He is not asking them to be disadvantaged in any way! As Karl Barth points out, Jesus stands equally above both husbands and wives as He stands equally below them. He is the Divine Original of both headship and servanthood. Barth beautifully encapsulates his thought: "He is the Exalted but also the Lowly, the Lowly but also the Exalted, who causes each to share in His glory but also His burden, His sovereignty but also His service."[10]

Are wives tempted, nonetheless, to resist subjection? Yes, and so are husbands tempted to turn headship into domineering and self-will. Each role must be transformed by grace. The formula of the paradox goes something like this—and I like the wording of David and Elouise Fraser—"Husbands, love your wives with Christ's love for the church (and thus be subject to

---

10. Karl Barth, *Church Dogmatics* III/2, tr. J. W. Edwards, O. Bussey, and Harold Knight (Edinburgh: T. & T. Clark, 1961), p. 313.

them and serve them); wives, be subject to your husbands as to Christ (and thus love them)."[11]

"But," some wife protests, "won't subjection sometimes bring too big a cost to me?" True, it might indeed. Look at Jesus; that is exactly what it brought Him! But if I hear a Christian wife agonizing about this, I have to wonder about her understanding of the Christian life. Is any Christian—man or woman—exempt from sharing the Lord's humiliation and suffering? Is this what the New Testament promises? We should be reminded once more that equal-partnership marriage is mutual subjection one to the other, and this means mutual sharing of the costs of servanthood. Yes, it will cost the wife something! Yes, it will cost the husband something! Everything worthwhile is costly, and the aims of Christian marriage being the highest of all, so the costs may well be commensurate with those aims and rewards.

Insofar as subjection causes a wife to be vulnerable to abuse at the hands of her husband, how he treats her will say much about him. He will be seen either as a caring, protecting lover, managing headship as God directs, or as a man who has not yet learned his own place of subjection to Christ, or the demands of love to which God has called him.

The key to full acceptance of the special vocation of subjection for wives is this: *it is a special gift and calling within a relationship of mutual servanthood.* To love and be loved, to serve and be served—this is the glory of God's design for Christian marriage!

---

11. David Fraser and Elouise Fraser, *Biblical View of Women* (unpublished manuscript), p. 57.

4 Mutual Servanthood: No Higher Goal!

In this final chapter on biblical roles for husbands and wives, our purpose is to bring together several strands of thought. We can now accept marriage as a partnership of equals, with two spouses each ministering mutually to the other in self-giving, Christlike love. This does not suggest, however, that we discard headship-subjection as the accepted framework within which this equal-partnership marriage operates. We've noted how the two are not at all incompatible. And neither can we suggest abolishing all sex roles on the basis of Galatians 3:28, as many are doing. Even less do we believe that this verse lends theological support to the disavowal of headship-subjection in marriage. The fact that a formidable segment of Christian feminists are urging such disavowal gives added reason to demonstrate exactly what Paul had in mind.

The Meaning of Galatians 3:28

The current debate includes those who teach that Galatians
3:28 eliminates altogether the traditional hierarchy of marital
authority taught by Paul elsewhere. Or if not altogether, they
say, at least his teaching here allows for inferences which permit
radical social change as Christianity advances. Such change, it is
claimed, would include moving from the old headship-subjection pattern to a modern equalitarian marriage. We are now in
such a time, presumably; it is incumbent upon us, therefore,
to bring about such a change.

What Galatians 3:28 says is this:

> There is neither Jew nor Greek, there is neither slave nor free,
> there is neither male nor female; for you are all one in Christ
> Jesus.

Paul Jewett calls this verse "The Magna Carta of Humanity."
One might easily contend that this is an overstatement. For one
thing, Paul's declaration is part of a discussion restricted entirely
to the church of the redeemed. He has just said in the two verses
preceding, "For in Christ Jesus you are all sons of God, through
faith. For as many of you as were baptized into Christ have put
on Christ." It is in the fellowship of believers, and only there,
that there is neither Jew nor Greek, slave nor free, male nor
female. They share the fact of unity in Christ; He is the source
and center of their unity. Here, then, in the church, is a major
social consequence of being a member of Christ's body: here
there is no spiritual distinction as to race, class, or sex. Whether
Paul intended that this spiritual unity become the ground for
arguing the abolition of sex roles is most questionable.

Despite chiding Paul Jewett for overstatement, I turn to him,
nevertheless, for an excellent statement of what Paul does mean
in Galatians 3:28:

> The thought of the apostle, then, must be that in Christ the basic
> divisions that have separated Man from his neighbor, divisions

which have threatened human fellowship, are done away. . . . Yet obviously these three categories are not alike in every respect. The distinction between slave and master is not a creation ordinance at all, but only a manifestation of Man's inhumanity to Man. It, then, is literally done away in Christ. The distinction between Jew and Greek, on the other hand, though hardly a creation ordinance, is consonant with creation, so long as it is not used to foster religious exclusivism and pride. It is done away in Christ, then, only insofar as it has been the occasion of divisions which separate Man from his fellow Man. Paul still considered himself a Jew (albeit a fulfilled one) rather than a Greek. As for male and female, this distinction represents, indeed, an ordinance of creation; Man has always been and always will be male and female because God created him so. Sexuality in a literal sense, then, is not abolished in Christ at all. In fact it should not even be suppressed. It is not sexuality but the immemorial antagonism between the sexes, perhaps the deepest and most subtle of all enmities, that is done away in him.[1]

What comes through loud and clear is that *what is abolished is sexual antagonisms, not sex roles!* And as to the particular inclusion of these three divisions, we are indebted to William Barclay for the following comment:

> There is something of very great interest here. In the Jewish form of morning prayer, which Paul must all his pre-Christian life have used, there is a thanksgiving in which the Jew thanks God that "Thou hast not made me a Gentile, a slave, or a woman." Paul takes that prayer and reverses it. The old distinctions are gone; for the disunity there is unity; for the separation there is communion; all are one in Christ.[2]

The comments of Herman Ridderbos are typical of the position taken in major commentaries. He first notes the context in which the words are found, showing that all sorts of people without any discrimination share in the grace of Christ. This is

---

1. Paul K. Jewett, *Man as Male and Female* (Grand Rapids: Eerdmans, 1975), p. 143.
2. William Barclay, *The Letters to the Galatians and Ephesians* (Philadelphia: Westminster Press, 1954), p. 35.

attested to, he says, by the fact that through faith all are sons of God, baptized into Christ. In Christ there are no distinctions by which to determine rank or status. But, Ridderbos cautions, "This is not to maintain that the natural and social distinction is in no respect relevant any more. . . . From the point of view of redemption in Christ, however, and of the gifts of the Spirit granted by Him, there is no preference of Jew to Greek, master to slave, man to woman."[3] None of these differences, in other words, are determinative of one's spiritual standing in Christ or position in the church. So far as the current debate is concerned, spiritual standing cannot be made to equate with social or sex roles.

Gordon Seminary professor John J. Davis addresses this question in response to the gratuitous position taken by feminist writers. I quote him at length:

> Clearly, Paul's intention in this passage is to establish a theological point, a point of soteriology, not to expound the proper social relationships of men and women in the Church. This he does notably in Colossians 3, Ephesians 5, and other passages . . . in the New Testament documents it is not assumed that equality in the sight of God implies either role interchangeability . . . or egalitarian authority patterns. . . . If one insists that the passage really teaches an egalitarian pattern for Christian marriage, then the analogy husband/wife–Christ/Church *would also negate the authority of Christ over the Church.* Surely this is an unacceptable result.[4] (italics added)

One of the arguments of the feminists is that Genesis 1:26–28 teaches that marriage originally was designed with an egalitarian pattern which subsequently was overturned by the fall. They see no incongruity in claiming that a hierarchical pattern

---

3. Herman Ridderbos, *Commentary on the Epistle of Paul to the Churches of Galatia*, in the *New International Commentary on the New Testament*, ed. F. F. Bruce (Grand Rapids: Eerdmans, 1953), p. 149.
4. John J. Davis, "Some Reflections on Galatians 3:28, Sexual Roles, and Biblical Hermeneutics," *Journal of the Evangelical Theological Society*, pp. 202–03.

cannot be inferred from Genesis 2:18–24, while at the same time insisting that an egalitarian pattern can indeed be inferred from Genesis 1:26–28. This requires a closer examination.

In answer to these claims, we contend that Genesis 2:18–24 at least indicates that woman was created subsequent to man, specifically to be his helper, to compensate for his loneliness; and by the inspired writer's own word she was created *for* (v. 18) as well as *from* (v. 22) man. Whatever weight we choose to give these considerations, they provide ground for claiming that the hierarchical pattern of marriage is *more appropriately affirmed than denied* on the basis of Genesis 2.

On the other hand, to claim an egalitarian marriage pattern on the ground that male and female were equally created in the image of God, and equally given dominion over the earth, is to equate *equal image* and *equal dominion* with *equal roles in marriage*. This is mixing apples with oranges, as well as flying in the face of the New Testament mandate in Ephesians and Colossians. Davis addresses this question:

> Granted, the rule of the husband over the wife in Genesis 3:16b is part of the curse inflicted on the woman, a curse presumably overcome in the redemptive economy. . . . But to draw completely egalitarian conclusions from this line of reasoning requires two further assumptions. The first is that in the redemptive economy the effects of sin are so completely eliminated that hierarchical authority patterns are no longer needed. The second assumption is that hierarchical authority structures exist only as a consequence of the Fall and were not part of the original creation order. *Neither assumption is adequately supported by the apostolic teaching . . .* inferring egalitarianism in marriage from Genesis 1:26–28 is something of an argument from silence because the passage has nothing direct to say about the specifics of the marriage relationship relative to the question of authority, either egalitarian or hierarchical . . . the joint exercise of dominion and joint image-bearing . . . [do] not establish egalitarianism with respect to every aspect of the relationship. Such a conclusion would be based on *the fallacious premise that equality in some respects entails equality in all respects.* Within the family relationship both parents and children

bear the image . . . but this does not establish symmetrical authority relationships between parents and children.[5] (italics added)

To argue for a radical change in the authority pattern of marriage on grounds of social inferences freely drawn from purely theological premises is fallacious. To do so in the face of what the same apostle says elsewhere about maintaining that very pattern is to prefer assumptions over contrary declarations.

Scripture makes it clear that we are to affirm our sexuality in all aspects of life, never denying it or seeking to transcend it. We are to rejoice in it as God's special gift, letting sexuality work for us, never against us. This does not mean, of course, that we are to stereotype the sexes into culturally shaped sex roles, or unjustly impose restrictions upon wives in the name of a false headship.

That there are even broader social implications than Paul intended, no one questions. What we do question is the assumption that this gives us license to oppose the apostle's theological word in Galatians to his own social implications in Ephesians and Colossians. No accepted biblical hermeneutic tolerates such a practice. It is distressing to see this principle unheeded in much of today's writing.

Achieving God's Order:
Headship-Subjection Within Equal Partnership

We're reminded once again that what makes marriage an equal partnership derives from the manner in which it is lived out, not the manner in which it is structured. Husbands and wives mutually serve one another in love; this is the vast difference that Christ makes. Now, if it seems difficult still to accept this paradox of hierarchy (headship-subjection) and equal partnership together, of order and freedom within the same

---

5. Ibid., p. 204.

design, then we need to be reminded of what Jesus said to His puzzled disciples in another connection: "Not all men can receive this precept, but only those to whom it is given" (Matt. 19:11). Christian spouses must be *enlightened* to the truth of the commands they have been given and *enabled* to carry those commands out. This is the work of the Holy Spirit. Nothing less than the transcendent power of Jesus Christ can bring about the happy fulfillment of this role-relationship. Of this we can be sure, however, that God will unfailingly grant success to every couple that permits Him to be Lord of their partnership.

Robert Capon sees an analogy between functional equality and ballet dancing. In the ballet, one dancer leads, the other follows—not because one is better (he may or may not be), but because that is his part. Here as elsewhere, it would be a mistake to think that equality is sameness, or that diversity of functions is irreconcilable with equal status or ability. The common notion of equality, says Capon, is based on the image of the march. In one form of marching—a parade—unequal persons are dressed alike, given guns of identical shape and length, trained to hold them at the same angle, and ordered to keep step with a fixed cadence. All are doing the same thing, and all look alike. But what is truer to life, Capon suggests, is not a parade but a dance. There people who are real equals are assigned unequal roles in order that each may achieve his individual perfection within the process as a whole. As nothing is less personal than a march, so nothing is more personal than a dance. It is here, in the dance, that we have fulfillment through unequal functions. Capon's word of counsel follows: "Keep that paradox and you move in the freedom of the dance; alter it, and you grow weary with marching."[6]

In a similar approach, Charlie Shedd suggests that marriage under the biblical order is like a conductor leading a symphony rather than a potentate ruling over his realm. While both illus-

---

6. Robert Farrar Capon, *Bed and Board: Plain Talk About Marriage* (New York: Simon and Schuster, 1965), p. 54.

trations are helpful, they are, of course, nothing more than reminders that leadership responsibility is to be understood largely as a role designed to serve—not some independent objective—but the purpose of the relationship itself.

What appears for the husband to be a position of power and prestige turns out to be almost the opposite! It is servanthood through committed love. And what about the wife? What appears to be a position of powerlessness turns out instead to be the creative power of servanthood. I think we can see the genius of God's design right here: *love is servanthood, and servanthood is love.* The Lord Jesus Christ teaches one how to take on either headship or subjection, as the case may be, through the power of His love.

Such love is always vulnerable, whether it be a husband's or a wife's. Love is always unprotected, always uncertain of achieving the ends to which it commits itself. It lives by faith and hope; this is the adventure of love. Remember, love is not merely the expression of an affectionate sentiment; it is an act of the will, a commitment of the entire person. As the much esteemed Bishop Westcott remarked, "The Church offers to Christ the devotion of subjection, as the wife to the husband. Christ offers to the Church the devotion of love, as the husband to the wife. Both are equal in self-surrender."[7]

It might be tempting to assume that we've been given a clever scheme where two people are both winners, and neither a loser. But since both partners give and both receive, in reality both win and both lose! Through both giving and receiving, winning and losing, a loving pair experience growth as persons as well as partners. God knew what He was doing when He locked these reciprocal roles into wedlock! And since both spouses are subject to Christ and to each other, they grow into wholeness. So whatever self-relinquishment is required, the highest rewards

---

7. Brooke Foss Westcott, *St. Paul's Epistle to the Ephesians* (Grand Rapids: Baker, 1979), p. 84.

are theirs. Best of all, the resources needed to fulfill the goal are available in Jesus Christ.

Now that we have established the basic principles, what may we expect as the cost husbands and wives will have to pay? Let's see if the *love-action of headship* and the *servant-action of subjection* really do generate the same end result. Let's explore how the husband's love might express itself, and at what cost to him. Then let's look at the wife's servanthood to see if it is similarly expressed, and at what cost to her.

As a backdrop, take Emile Verhaeren's declaration, ''With the whole of my being I love the whole of your being.'' This is a goal husbands might adopt. And what about wives? We might substitute one word and say for wives, ''With the whole of my being I *serve* the whole of your being.''

From the very beginning, Scripture takes a holistic view of man and a complementary view of relationships. This is most importantly true of marriage, the most intimate and demanding of all human relationships. To affirm another person in marriage is to affirm all that he or she is and is becoming. How different this is from affirming what we wish the other were! On the husband's part, his love is to set his wife free to grow in her individuality and self-actualization. He enables her to experience wholeness as a person as well as a partner. No other design could better assure her fulfillment as a woman. On her part, loving servanthood sets her husband free to take his responsibility seriously, thereby experiencing growth for himself both as man and as husband. As love is other-affirming, so is servanthood, and the cost to each mate is the same.

It seems perfectly natural that no loving husband would want anything less than for his wife to become a fulfilled person. Nor would he ever want her to be in subjection simply for subjection's sake. From her standpoint as a wife whose life is grounded in Christ, she is not out to make her goal self-fulfillment. That must come as a subsidiary development. She accepts servanthood as a denial of self. Thus, self-fulfillment cannot be the end of her existence. Yet, paradoxically, a loving husband desires nothing less for her. So what a godly wife will not choose for her own goal, her husband chooses as his goal for her.

When one spouse is fulfilling his or her role, the partner's desire and ability to do the same are enhanced. For one encourages the other. Just as the wife's subjection enhances her husband's capacity to love—by providing the added motivation of gratefulness—so, in like manner, his love in action enhances her subjection, for she, too, has the added motivation of the same gratefulness. So, you see, whatever the initial starting point, whether that of husband or wife, a single quality of reciprocity emerges—*self-giving, Christlike love expressing itself through mutual servanthood.* To lovingly serve, and to be lovingly served, this is the greatness of God's design!

All this is not to say that mutual subjection involves equal give-and-take, much less that it stands for something that can be calculated. Marriage isn't a bookkeeping arrangement! The requirement of any given situation will rest unequally upon the partners. This is as it should be in a relationship based on complementarity, where individual need and ability vary with time and circumstance. Within a loving relationship, a just and proper division of responsibilities will develop in time. The ultimate responsibility which falls upon the husband as head is to see that fairness prevails in the unequal give-and-take. He is responsible to see that marital well-being is served.

Karl Barth points out that the husband who is obedient to God's plan will not leave it to happenstance whether or not the marriage order gets established and continues in a healthy way. On the contrary, he will accept responsibility for the communion of marriage all along the way, from its earliest beginnings. To have primary concern for the order itself is his ultimate responsibility. To the extent that he is vigilant for their common interests, he will be strong. Correspondingly, the wife too will desire the establishment and continuance of God's order. This is made easier as she realizes that her own individuality and growth—even her special interests—are best secured within God's design. She will feel neither a sense of inferiority nor an impulse to jealousy. Far from any feeling of being deprived, she will consider her welfare promoted and protected. What an unfettered opportunity to develop her potential to its fullest! With her worthiness reinforced by her husband's loving concern, she is truly free to become all she's meant to be!

Unquestionably, subjection renders a wife vulnerable in the face of her husband's superior position of headship. But is it not equally true that the demands of love make a husband just as vulnerable to his wife? Yes, indeed! For love is willingness to reach out from where one is with what one has, and in the process to take personal risks for the beloved's sake. Love opens itself to the needs of another, not calculating the cost to oneself. It is willing to move unprotected into all areas of another's need, even, if necessary, to suffer misunderstanding, rebuff, or rejection. By its very nature, love cannot close itself off, or protect itself once it has taken the step to care. Thus, when we say that subjection is vulnerability, we must recognize that love invites an equal vulnerability. Not that we haven't experienced plenty of the former; we need now to see equal demonstrations of the latter.

The supreme example of love's vulnerability shall always be Christ's death on the cross; His love risked and suffered all. So the model of Christ as *Head* and as *Servant*—equally majestic—demands an equal willingness of both spouses to be vulnerable to each other. Is this too great a cost for loving servanthood?

Dealing with a Partner Who Fails to Fulfill God's Order

In a practical sense, the ability of either spouse to fulfill his or her role is somewhat dependent upon the other's doing the same. Does this mean, then, that one has an obligation to his mate only insofar as the mate fulfills his or her role? There are no conditional clauses in Ephesians 5 or its parallel in Colossians.

The nature of God's command is unconditional. Husbands are commanded to love their wives regardless of the wife's subjection. Similarly, wives are to be subject to their husbands regardless of the husband's love. Neither partner is free to disregard his role because of the disobedience of the other. Marriage commitment has no escape clauses!

It is here that we can see the liberating effect of our being responsible to the Lord for ourselves. One can never excuse his own disobedience by pointing to the other's failure, for it is to the Lord alone that each spouse is accountable. Fidelity to one's own role is first of all fidelity to Jesus Christ and His special call. And the model for obedience is the Lord, not one's marriage partner. If at times this means we must take a difficult road, then we are to remember our model, the One whose obedience led to Calvary, but whose reward for obedience was enthronement in heaven. *Follow Him!*

Suppose, now, that one partner does refuse, or neglect, to fulfill his or her role. What is the other to do? If we grant that communication is basic to the development of all relationships, we should allow the tested spouse to freely express a legitimate complaint to the erring mate. There is no reason to believe that such a course is contrary to the spirit of subjection. God may use either mate to teach the other.

It may be necessary, for example, for a wife to say, "Dear, I do so want to be in subjection to you in all things as to the Lord, but you are making it very difficult by your lack of loving responsibility. With the Lord's strength I shall seek to fulfill my role as a truly subject wife, and I am praying that God will enable you to fulfill your headship as He directs." If she says this lovingly and follows it up with actions which demonstrate her earnestness, the wife may influence her husband to an acknowledgment of failure, or at least of desire to meet the challenge—perhaps to his requesting her prayers and help.

Or it may be necessary for a husband to say, "Dear, I truly want to fulfill my responsibility of loving headship in our marriage, but you are making it all but impossible by your independence and lack of cooperation. I shall seek to do my best with the Lord's help, and I am praying that you will find it in your heart to take the place He has appointed for you. I believe there are greater growth and happiness ahead for both of us."

Should we not expect the Holy Spirit to be pleased to use such approaches, not so much as prods but encouragements? Of course, one must not come across as though delivering a stinging rebuke or expressing a purely resentful reaction. It should always be evident that a mate is humbly expressing a longing for God's best. And such will be the case if one approaches the situation with sensitivity and prayer.

Characteristic of the dominating husband, as opposed to one who is strong yet spiritually obedient, is his attempt to make the order serve himself, rather than his serving the order. Perhaps no sinful disorder is more subtle, more easily exploited, and more tempting, than male domination. God's order is abused almost unknowingly to support the misapprehension that God Himself has given man some kind of advantage over his wife. Appealing to his natural desire for dominance, headship is changed into a means of seizing and exerting power over another. For sure, the two spouses are one—*and he's the one!*

Should a husband become domineering, his wife may make the mistake of obliging him, becoming a compliant, accommodating mate. In going along with such behavior, perhaps seeming to invite its continuance, she may subject herself—but in a very mistaken way. She may play the part which her domineering husband desires, which he needs in order to feel successful. In this way, peace is maintained, but only by accommodation and appeasement.

That there is no conflict in this marriage is due only to the wife's having chosen the way of self-negation. She is willing to be a nonperson, perhaps because this is what she has been led to believe is proper subjection. So she says nothing, seeks to discover in advance what is expected of her, and fulfills it to the letter. All the while she congratulates herself for contributing to the stabilization and peace of their marriage.

Look more closely. You see that such a wife is only playing a part. She has no real existence of her own, no true place in the order, and is contributing to an abuse of the order. She is but a corresponding example of disobedience. Certain it is that her kind of subjection will not help her husband master his desire for domination. She can be an agent of change if she so desires.

Whenever a wife chooses to take this unlikely form of losing herself in order to save herself, she suffers deep injury. It is only a matter of time before she realizes how she has been used. The disorder will have severe consequences on her own behavior. Eventually, disillusioned, perhaps broken, she will seek at last to extricate herself from this newly recognized bondage. The sad thing is that she will then question not only her husband's lording it over her, but the whole biblical order itself.

Christian husbands and wives are called to a beautiful complementarity of roles, to a marvelously designed symmetry of loving service to each other. Each has a distinctive starting point, a unique role. Each has distinctive strengths which may be employed in special ministries to the other. Each is called to model the majesty and lowliness of the Lord Jesus Christ—one as *head* and the other as *servant*. For the husband this means headship responsibly exercised by means of self-giving love. For the wife this means subjection responsibly exercised by means of self-giving servanthood. For the two there is a renunciation of all personal claims, all rights, in favor of an enduring commitment to loving service. Both roles have a corresponding dignity and honor, for both equally entitle their bearers to bring highest glory to the Savior. To love Him is to love the order He has appointed for marital harmony and happiness. This order represents and witnesses to the relation between Christ and the church. These roles are God's command; *they are also His gift!*[8]

---

8. The reader who wishes to do further study is encouraged to consult David Martyn Lloyd-Jones, *Life in the Spirit: In Marriage, Home, and Work* (Grand Rapids: Baker, 1973); and two articles by A. Duane Litfin, "A Biblical View of the Marital Roles: Seeking a Balance," *Bibliotheca Sacra*, vol. 133, no. 532 (Oct.–Dec. 1976), pp. 330–37; and "Evangelical Feminism: Why Traditionalists Reject It," *Bibliotheca Sacra*, vol. 136, no. 543 (July–Sept. 1979), pp. 258–71.